LIVING

AS A YOUNG WOMAN OF GOD

JEN RAWSON

D0580391

ZONDERVAN®

ZONDERVAN.com/
AUTHORTRACKER
follow your favorite authors

youth specialties

**youth
specialties**

Living as a Young Woman of God
Copyright 2008 by Jen Rawson

Youth Specialties resources, 300 S. Pierce St., El Cajon, CA 92020 are published by Zondervan, 5300 Patterson Ave. SE, Grand Rapids, MI 49530.

ISBN 978-0-310-27548-0

Web site addresses listed in this book were current at the time of publication. Please contact Youth Specialties via e-mail (YS@YouthSpecialties.com) to report URLs that are no longer operational and replacement URLs if available.

Cover design by Toolbox Studios
Interior design by Mark Novelli, IMAGO MEDIA

Printed in the United States of America

12 13 • 20 19 18 17 16 15 14 13 12 11 10 9 8 7 6 5

My beauty from the ashes.

Dedicated to the most important girls in my life. Clera, Charis, Hannah, Alexis, Caroline, and Lillian.

A special thanks to my mom, Rita Harris, for being my example of becoming and living as a godly woman.

CONTENTS

INTRODUCTION: WHY YOU NEED THIS BOOK

It's amazingly easy to convince a middle school girl that she's worthless, that her parents don't understand her, and that everything about her is inadequate. She may be transformed from a girl who a few years prior loved many things and was confident and mostly pleasant to be around into an emotional, dramatic young woman who's obsessed with her appearance and no longer believes in herself. How does this happen? The answer is quite simple. Our culture—with its television, magazines, movies, music, billboards, and the Internet—combined with the pressures of school life and girls' changing bodies, minds, and emotions is a mixture sure to confuse and upset even the most foundationally stable girls. They stop being themselves and start appearing and acting like all the other females around them. They take on the rigorous occupation of evolving into the "ideal woman" by being female impersonators. Then when they see they're failing at the task of becoming ideal women (because they all will), their lives become a mess. What's more, parents are often on their own in this struggle. And when parental advice goes up against the views of friends and the media, guess whose suggestions and concerns are left by the wayside?

Living as a Young Woman of God is designed to help girls stop pretending and start living as the young women God created them to be. When they embrace and stay true to that identity, your girls not only will survive this tumultuous transition into womanhood, but they'll also be happy, healthy, and whole. *Living as a Young Woman of God* creates an opportunity for you to come alongside parents to mentor girls in the face of our culture and the lies it tells them. It helps you train girls to use the minds God gave them to question and critique what they're seeing, hearing, and reading. It upholds truth—because girls must find value in who they are, *as* they are; exude authenticity; and have the courage and know-how to analyze life instead of let life happen to them.

WHAT IT IS

Living as a Young Woman of God is an eight-week curriculum geared toward a small group of middle school girls being discipled by adult women. It addresses the nuts-and-bolts, practical aspects of thriving in life as a young woman of God, including caring for their relationships, finding true value and worth, dealing with their emotions, and appreciating their bodies inside and out. It continues the process (begun in *Becoming a Young Woman of God*) of transforming their thinking from a mentality that values what our culture says to the mind of Christ. From trying to be like all the women, they move to trying to become like Christ.

The goal is for your girls to discover and appreciate how great it is that they're *not* like every other girl out there and to stay on track in the journey toward living as the women God wants them to be, toward finding their value in Jesus. If your girls can internalize the truth that they're valuable because God created and cares about them, as well as use their minds to process and question what they see and hear, they'll be on track for healthy choices and fulfilling lives. They'll see themselves as truly beautiful because they're living like Christ.

THE METHOD BEHIND THE MADNESS

Ingredients

At the beginning of each lesson you'll find a list of items you'll need to lead the session.

Appetizer

Each session begins with a crazy game or activity that ties into the topic for the week. Sometimes the point is made right away; other times the point of the game/activity is brought up later in the session. When it comes to games, most middle school girls are up for about anything. But occasionally a girl doesn't want to participate. In these cases I always encourage the girl but never force her. If the same girl doesn't want to participate every week, have one of your more mature students personally invite her to get involved. (An invitation from an adult isn't the same as one from a peer.)

Specialty

Each session incorporates activities such as fun quizzes and group projects, age-appropriate crafts, situation scenarios, movie clips, music, and stories. To keep interest high, most sessions include the option of using at least one video clip.

Time limit disclaimer: You may not have the necessary minutes or hours to get through all of the activities in each session from week to week. That's okay! If there's more than one movie clip, and you don't have time for both, just choose the one you like better. The same is true for the other activities. Pick and choose whatever best gets through to your group. If a craft doesn't go well one week, try something else the next. On a low budget? Check out books and movies from the library. Do what works for you.

Take Out

At the end of most sessions, there's a suggested way for the girls to take home what they've learned that day. This is an object of some kind that they can place in their rooms, in their pockets, or in their lockers at school; it will remind them of the truth you all discussed. (What your girls are learning goes against what our culture is teaching them; changing our minds isn't easy. So they need all the reminders they can get!)

Notes to Parents

I believe our role as leaders is to assist parents. They know their children better than anyone else, and you get the opportunity to assist the experts in molding these girls. So in a few lessons we ask parents to get involved, sometimes by helping their daughters with the brainteasers and Soul Work questions and sometimes through letters you'll send to the parents. You'll need to check ahead of time which weeks include notes to parents, as these must be mailed to give parents enough time to respond during those weeks.

Reality Check (student outlines)

To help your girls stay focused there are reproducible student outlines to pass out to them before each session. The outlines can help your girls remain actively involved in the session as they follow along, fill in the blanks, and answer multiple choice questions, as well as group questions. Plus, when they put pens to paper, they're taking one more step toward cementing truth in their hearts and minds. The student outlines will also be very helpful for the girls during the week while they're doing their **Soul Work**.

(Note: As you're leading the session and come to a "Reality Check" heading, just prompt your girls by saying "Reality Check" and ask the question or questions or read the statement or verse— your girls have the same wording on their handouts.)

Also, make sure your girls save their Reality Check outlines from week to week—they'll all help with the Final Project, should you choose to have them do it.

Soul Work

This is a fancy word for *homework*—but because it's homework for the soul, it's much more meaningful than studying for a math quiz. **Soul Work** is done during the week, between meetings. It includes assignments such as interviews, journaling, and many other activities that help your girls think for themselves.

Each **Soul Work** handout starts out with some fun brainteasers that seem to have nothing to do with anything. But you can be assured they do have a purpose. First, they help the girls look forward to something; second, they encourage them to talk to their parents and siblings about the answers. (Pretty tricky, eh?)

Plus, every week each girl is asked to be in contact with an "other" to reinforce her relationships with parents, grandparents, and mentors. The "other" typically is Mom—a middle school girl's hardest relationship is with her mom. Yet it's by far one of the most important, so we want to help as much as we can to foster that relationship. If we're lucky enough to catch moms and daughters when they aren't struggling with communication, then it will make the relational foundation all the more firm—and will further aid your girls to deal with what's to come.

You'll have some girls who are faithful in doing their **Soul Work** every week; others may never do a single assignment. When girls come with their **Soul Work** incomplete, rather than laying on the guilt, help them through the discussion. And keep encouraging them to do the work since it will allow them to see how what they've learned meets real life, covers material you didn't have time to deal with at the meeting, and helps them get personal and application-oriented with regard to the study sessions. You can review the answers and thoughts the girls came up with—just keep in mind how much time you want to spend reviewing a previous week's **Soul Work** versus leading the current session.

Also, make sure your girls save their Soul Work sheets from week to week—they'll all help with the Final Project, should you choose to have them do it.

ONE LAST THOUGHT

You're about to embark on a trip that few women take part in. Middle school students are often forgotten. They're not children but far from adults. They're moody, mouthy...and yet moldable. Their minds are switching from concrete to abstract. They're just starting to question what's real and what isn't. Do they really believe in this God their parents believe in? They're trying to decide which friends they're going to hang around. Most important, they're trying to discover who they are and who they're going to become.

That's when you step in.

CHAPTER ONE

LIVING AS MY S.E.L.F.

INGREDIENTS

Paper and crayons, Polaroid camera, pictures children have drawn and signed their names on, *Toy Story* DVD, pictures of a chameleon, *Napoleon Dynamite* DVD, Polaroid camera

REVIEW SOUL WORK (OPTION)

Assuming you're transitioning with your girls from *Becoming a Young Woman of God*, answer to the brainteaser from chapter eight of that book: The big car was a hearse.

APPETIZER: VANITY PLATES

When students arrive, have paper and crayons out for them to start creating their own license plates. Their goal is to create plates that describe or fit them—that's to say, if they were to get vanity plates when they can drive, what would the plates say? Share some examples you've seen or yours if you've ever had one: KLULESS, N LUV, SWEET16, GODZKUL. Allot as much time as you need to take photos (see next paragraph) or to play one song of your choice.

While your girls are creating their vanity plates, take a Polaroid photo of each girl. If you don't have a Polaroid camera, you have a few options here. You can use a digital camera and send an assistant to a computer to print out a copy of each girl's photo. If you don't have a digital camera, use a regular one; and if you can't spare another adult, just print out the pictures later and mail them this week.

Let the girls share their vanity plates. Commend them on their creativity and tell them you'd like to share some examples of creativity your children (or children you know) made.

Bring in a couple of pictures or projects your children (or someone else's children) have created and signed. Show them to the students and say, **If I had a painting and said it was by Leonardo da Vinci, how would you know I was being honest? His name would be on it.**

(And I'd be really, really, really wealthy.) The artist's name is what brings value to a piece of artwork. Who cares if I try to paint the *Mona Lisa*? Even if it looked exactly like the original, it wouldn't be worth a cent. It has to have one name on it—and it's not mine.

Point at the children's artwork and say, **These will never hang in an art museum. No one will ever give me thousands of dollars for these. But they do have one thing in common with every famous painting in existence. They have value because of one thing.** Point to the "signatures" and read them. Say, **These pieces of paper have value because of the names on them.**

QUESTIONS AND COMMENTARY

Specialty: Movie Clip

Show *Toy Story* clip (56:00 - 59:10: Andy and Buzz are trying to escape Sid's room; Buzz has given up on himself because he's figured out he's only a toy; Woody tries to cheer him up by telling him how great he is because of his buttons and lights; and Buzz decides he's valuable because Andy writes his name on Buzz).

Ask, **Who made you?** After some answers say, **Psalm 139 tells us that God made us.**

Reality Check

1. If God made you, then whose name is written on you?

After some answers, say, **God's. God's name on you makes you valuable. You're a masterpiece.**

Show a couple of pictures you found on the Internet or in a book of a chameleon in different settings. Then say, **Like a chameleon, you often try to blend in and change to match every person you're around. Most girls do. But while God had the power to create you to be a chameleon, God chose not to. What makes you so great is, you're different from everyone else! You're unique, extraordinary, and irreplaceable. You're special and one of a kind. Why would you try to be like everyone else?**

Say, **We're amazed at the idea that no two snowflakes are alike or no two fingerprints are alike. Even twins who look identical are different in some way. Yet we have a problem being different—**

being ourselves—and we fight as hard as we can to be like every-one else.

Continue, **God spent time making you. God chose your hair type and color, your eye color, height, and all kinds of physical things about you. Yet we often try to become like everyone else, and we're upset or stressed out about not being as athletic, creative, grace-ful, outgoing, or intelligent as others. But the reality is…**

Reality Check

2. We try to be like others, but we weren't created to be like ev-eryone else—so we're fighting a battle we can't win. We need to embrace our S.E.L.F.

Have your girls circle *created* and *S.E.L.F.* Then say, **I bet you've heard about "looking at the heart instead of the outward appear-ance." Usually, people say it when talking about others and how to treat them. But what does that mean for you?** After some answers say, **Many things make you who you are besides the obvious out-ward things.**

Reality Check

3. God created a whole unique system <u>inside</u> you. This is who God intended for you to become.

Say, **As you're discovering who God intends you to become, you'll see more clearly what God intends for you to do with the rest of your life. 1 Corinthians 10:31 tells us, "So whether you eat or drink or whatever you do, do it all for the glory of God." We were created to have a relationship with God and to show God's glory. What do you think that means—to "show God's glory"?**

After some answers say, **It means…**

Reality Check

4. We need to make the invisible God visible to others. God gave each of you your own way of doing that. You need to <u>understand</u> how God made you so you can <u>accept</u> yourself and do what you were created for.

Explain the acronym S.E.L.F. to the group.

Reality Check

5. Skills, experience, likes, and foundation (S.E.L.F.) are four of the biggest things God has given you—they form who you are today.

Then say, **This is a way for you to remember your inside parts. Let's look at the big canvas God has filled into a masterpiece called YOU.**

> **Skills**:
>
> ▷ **anything I'm really, REALLY good at**
>
> ▷ **natural talents**
>
> ▷ **abilities**

Specialty: Movie Clip

Show *Napoleon Dynamite* clip (35:21-36:00) in which Napoleon tells Pedro about his "skills"—for example, computer hacking skills, nun-chuck skills, etc.

Then say, **Skills are the things you're really, really good at. These are your natural talents and abilities. They're often what people compliment you on. God has made you good at things others may or may not be good at...and vice versa. Tell the person on your left one skill you have.** (It may help get the ball rolling if you share a fun personal story of a skill you have now or had in middle school.)

Reality Check

6. Experience:

We make <u>good choices</u> and bad choices. Sometimes good things happen to us, and sometimes <u>bad</u> things happen. Everything that happens to us (by our choice or not) forms a little more of who we are.

Leader Note: *This is a hard topic so make sure your students know you're available to them if they need to talk about anything. Also make sure to mention that when bad things, such as abuse and divorce, etc., happen, it's not their fault, and they may need to get some help.*

This may bring up the question "Why do bad things happen to good people?" Or "Why does God make bad things happen?" Or "Why does God allow bad things to happen?" This is a whole lesson in itself. Make sure they know to come next week to find out more!

If they ask, say, **The short answer for now is: It's hard to say whether God makes things happen or allows them to happen—but either way, they happen. It's always fine to hurt, to cry, to be angry; God can handle our questions and our frustrations. God's biggest goal in any bad or hard situation is to bring good from it and make our relationship with God stronger. We need to remember, what we think is best isn't always what God thinks is best. We have a choice in every situation—to become a stronger person and rise above the circumstances or let them take us down.**

Say, **Whether bad or good things happen to us, they help make us who we are. Our parents form who we are. If we're chosen for some huge honor, that forms who we are. If we're abused, we're formed in some way; if we're in an accident, that helps form us; if we grow up on a farm or in the city, that forms us; if we go on a mission trip, that forms us.**

Share an experience that's formed who you are. Then ask for some volunteers to share their own experiences.

Reality Check

7. Likes:

These are the things you love to do.

Say, **These can be different from things you're good at—your skills. You just enjoy doing your "likes," whether you're good at them or not. What makes you feel joy? What are you doing when you feel most alive? What are you passionate about? God instilled these things in you.**

Now say, **Tell the person to your right one thing you like to do.**

After that quick moment of sharing, say, **If you want to build a building to last, you need a firm foundation. The farther up you want your building to rise, the farther down you need to build it into the ground. As a tree grows and becomes stronger, its roots grow larger, going deeper into the ground and forming a founda-**

tion that won't let the tree fall over. Ask, **How did God create us similar to trees or buildings?**

After some answers say, **God has given us a foundation for our lives.**

Reality Check

8. Foundation:

Your foundation is your <u>personality</u>.

Say, **The basics of your self are wrapped up in your personality. The ways you act around others, make decisions, carry out everyday life, and relate to others are all because of this foundation, your personality. Your actions stem from your personality. Like a tree, you can stand strong as an individual because of this foundation.**

Say, **Four basic roots form this foundation.**

Leader Note: *These characteristics are based on the Myers-Briggs personality types, but section D is different—it relates more to someone in middle school who's trying to become an independent individual and discovering new insights about herself. Explain these to your girls.*

Reality Check

A. Introvert or extrovert: This is the way you <u>act</u> around other people.

Say, **Introverted people tend to have a few close friends with very deep relationships. They don't mind being by themselves and are usually the quiet ones in a group of people. Some don't like big groups; others don't mind them but feel drained after being with lots of people. Some have just a hint of introversion while others are so introverted they can be mistaken for being snobs.**

Continue, **Extroverted people tend to have a lot of friends, though most of the relationships may not be deep. They don't tend to enjoy being alone. They love to be in big groups and are usually the ones doing most of the talking. Instead of being exhausted after being around lots of people, they tend to have even more energy. Some are just a little extroverted and enjoy people where**

others are so extremely extroverted they can be mistaken for being obnoxious.

Reality Check

B. Thinking or feeling: This is the way you make <u>decisions</u>.

Now say, **Thinkers want to know all the facts. They weigh the pros and cons. They consider past outcomes and want to know every possible outcome of a decision before they make one. They tend to see everything as it is, without imagining extra information. They pay attention to detail. They stick to what makes sense. They often notice what people are wearing and which decorations are on the wall. Think of these people as information sponges.**

Then say, **Feelers are good dreamers and visionaries. They think of possibilities that haven't happened yet. They don't seem as concerned about the past. They're not worried if something has never been done before. They tend to miss small details. They usually have great imaginations. They often base their decisions on their gut feelings or on hunches. They may miss what someone's wearing but are good at noticing how someone's feeling inside.**

Reality Check

C. Structured or spontaneous: This is the way you carry out your day—your <u>actions</u>.

Say, **Structured people are organized. They like to-do lists, calendars, and schedules. They have everything planned out and enjoy working with deadlines. They like things to be in all the right places and in order. Change is often hard for structured people.**

Now say, **Spontaneous people like change. They sometimes need change so they don't go crazy. They don't worry about planning ahead because plans change. They don't want to make a to-do list because they feel they have plenty of time to get it all done—they'll eventually get around to things.**

Reality Check

D. Dependent or independent: This is the way you <u>relate</u> to people.

Explain, **Dependent people rely on others' opinions, and they need approval from others. They tend to expect a lot from others and rely on others to help them through difficult situations. They need to talk with others to sort out their feelings.**

Then say, **Independent people rely on their own opinions and count on themselves to get through tough situations. They usually have high expectations of themselves but worry little about others. They often need to be alone to sort through their feelings.**

Reality Check

9. The hard thing about these different sides of our personalities is we often think of one side as right or strong and the other as wrong or weak. The reality is, neither is better than the other.

Tell the girls, **Circle *strong* and *weak*. The other hard thing about personalities is, while some of us are very obviously one side or the other, others border on both.**

Say, **No matter which qualities you have, your personality is how God made you. It can help you understand why you're exhausted and ready to be alone even when you're with your best friends—you're introverted; why it takes you much longer than others to make a decision—you're a thinker; why you get so frustrated when your plans get changed without warning—you're structured; or why you can't seem to let go of what others think of you—you're dependent.** (To illustrate, describe aspects of your own personality and how it falls into these categories.)

Continue, **This week you're going to look at your S.E.L.F. and see how God created you. If you're able to understand how God created your personality, you can use that information to become as strong and successful as possible.**

Now say, **By understanding your S.E.L.F., you can begin to fall in love with who God made you to be. Just as a lion is still a lion even without its teeth, you can try to act differently, but you usually won't change who you are. If you're an introverted person, you can try to be the life of the party, but it probably won't feel right to you. You won't enjoy it. Likewise if you're an extroverted person, you can try to be quieter and get energized by spending time alone, but you may find you become very lonely. You're a creation specially designed by God just the way you are.**

Say, **You're valuable because God's name is on you. Your life can be a big thank-you card you live out. You can be thankful for how God created you when you embrace your S.E.L.F. Stop fighting to be someone else and learn how to be the best S.E.L.F you can.**

TAKE OUT

Have each girl write S E L F on the back of their vanity plates to remind them of how they want others to describe them—and how they should be presenting themselves to others.

Give each girl a Polaroid picture or digital print of herself. On the bottom of the picture in the white spot or on the back, have each student write GOD. Tell the girls they're valuable because God's name is on them. God made them, and God made who they are on the inside, too. If you can't get a Polaroid or can't spare a helper with the digital camera, you can still pull this off—just mail each girl a print this week with a little note telling her why she's valuable.

Distribute **Soul Work** handouts and close in prayer.

REALITY CHECK

LIVING AS MY S.E.L.F.

1. If God made you, then whose name is written on you?

2. We try to be like others, but we weren't created to be like everyone else—so we're fighting a battle we can't win. We need to embrace our S.E.L.F.

3. God created a whole unique system inside you. This is who God intended for you to become.

4. We need to make the invisible God visible to others. God gave each of you your own way of doing that. You need to _____ how God made you so you can _____ yourself and do what you were created for.

5. Skills, experience, likes, and foundation (S.E.L.F.) are four of the biggest things God has given you—they form who you are today.

   _____ :

   ▷ anything I'm really, REALLY good at

   ▷ natural talents

   ▷ abilities

6. Experience:

   We make _____ and bad choices. Sometimes good things happen to us, and sometimes _____ things happen. Everything that happens to us (by our choice or not) forms a little more of who we are.

7. _____:

   These are the things you love to do.

8. Foundation:

   Your foundation is your _____.

   A. Introvert or extrovert: This is the way you _____ around other people.

   B. Thinking or feeling: This is the way you make _____.

   C. Structured or spontaneous: This is the way you carry out your day—your _____.

   D. Dependent or independent: This is the way you _____ to people.

9. The hard thing about these different sides of our personalities is we often think of one side as right or strong and the other as wrong or weak. The reality is, neither is better than the other.

SOUL WORK

LIVING AS MY S.E.L.F

Brainteasers

Time to start those brains!

1. If you had a match and entered a room in which there was a kerosene lamp, an oil heater, and a wood-burning stove, which would you light first?

2. Why can't a man living in Wichita, Kansas, be buried in Florida?

3. Some months have 30 days and some months have 31 days; how many have 28?
   _____

4. How far can a dog run into the woods?

5. A farmer had 17 sheep, and all but nine died. How many does he have left?
   _____

Soul Work questions

You girls have done such a great job so far. You've been working hard, and I hope you're discovering things you'd never thought of before. This week we'll be looking at some fun things about YOU.

1. What makes you valuable?

2. What's the acronym to help you remember that wonderful, unique internal system God has given you—the part of you that's who you are intended to be?

   (HINT: Look at your Reality Check sheet or even just at the next question.)

3. What do each of the letters stand for?

   S _____

   E _____

   L _____

   F _____

4. Skills are what you're really, really good at. I want you to list as many things as you can think of that you're really, really good at. You can add to this list all week long as you think of more and more. Skills can include things such as sports, music, subjects in school, drawing, memory, encouraging, cooking, gardening, writing, planning, entertaining, photography, teaching, compassion, giving, listening, making phone calls—anything at all. You could also ask a friend for her thoughts about this.

5. What are some experiences—good and bad—that have shaped who you are today?

6. Likes are things you absolutely love to do. These can include many of the same things as your skills, though they aren't always the same. Likes can be things such as watching movies, reading, eating out, playing games, sleeping, babysitting, talking on the phone, etc.

7. Foundation is the core of who you are, your personality. The basics of who you are are wrapped up in your personality. The way you act around others, make a decision, carry out your everyday life, and relate to others are all foundations of your personality. Your actions stem from your personality. Circle the one in each pair that fits you—or both if you're right in the middle.

A. Introvert or extrovert: This is the way you act around other people.

Introverted people tend to have a few close friends with very deep relationships. They don't mind being by themselves and are usually the quiet ones in a group of people. Some don't like big groups; others don't mind them but feel drained after being with lots of people. Some have just a hint of introversion while others are so introverted they can be mistaken for being snobs.

Extroverted people tend to have a lot of friends, though most of the relationships may not be deep. They don't tend to enjoy being alone. They love to be in big groups and are usually the ones doing most of the talking. Instead of being exhausted after being around lots of people, they tend to have even more energy. Some are just a little extroverted and enjoy people where others are so extremely extroverted they can be mistaken for being obnoxious.

B. Thinking or feeling: This is the way you make decisions.

Thinkers want to know all the facts. They weigh the pros and cons. They consider past outcomes and want to know every possible outcome of a decision before they make one. They tend to see everything as it is, without imagining extra information. They pay attention to detail. They stick to what makes sense. They often notice what people are wearing and which decorations are on the wall. Think of these people as information sponges.

Feelers are good dreamers and visionaries. They think of possibilities that haven't happened yet. They don't seem as concerned about the past. They're not worried if something has never been done before. They tend to miss small details. They usually have great imaginations. They often base their decisions on their gut feelings or on hunches. They may miss what someone's wearing but are good at noticing how someone's feeling inside.

C. Structured or spontaneous: This is the way you carry out your day—your actions.

Structured people are organized. They like to-do lists, calendars, and schedules. They have everything planned out and enjoy working with deadlines. They like things to be in all the right places and in order. Change is often hard for structured people.

Spontaneous people like change. They sometimes need change so they don't go crazy. They don't worry about planning ahead because plans change. They don't want to make a to-do list because they feel they have plenty of time to get it all done—they'll eventually get around to things.

D. Dependent or independent: This is the way you relate to people.

Dependent people rely on others' opinions, and they need approval from others. They tend to expect a lot from others and rely on others to help them through difficult situations. They need to talk with others to sort out their feelings.

Independent people rely on their own opinions and count on themselves to get through tough situations. They usually have high expectations of themselves but worry little about others. They often need to be alone to sort through their feelings.

CHAPTER TWO

LIVING WHOLE: DEALING WITH PAIN AND DISAPPOINTMENT

INGREDIENTS

Pennies (about 10 per girl), *Superman* DVD

REVIEW SOUL WORK

Answers to the brainteasers:

1. The match
2. Because he's alive
3. All of them
4. Halfway—after that he's running *out* of the woods
5. Nine

APPETIZER: "I NEVER"

You'll need a lot of pennies for this game. Each student will need approximately 10. Sit in a circle and start by stating one thing you've never done. For example, I've never had my hair cut shorter than chin length. I've never traveled outside the U.S. I've never ridden on a train. Everyone who *has* done the activity gives you a penny. Go around so everyone gets a chance to say one thing they've never done. Whoever has the most pennies at the end of the game wins all the pennies.

After the game say, **We all have things we've done and things we've never done. Some things we do every day shape us, and some things others do *to* us every day shape us.**

QUESTIONS AND COMMENTARY

Reality Check

1. **All the <u>experiences</u> in our lives shape who we are.**

Say, **Last week we talked about how God made us. Experiences aren't ways God made you but what life has done to you.**

Reality Check

2. **We're all surrounded by good and evil. We make <u>good</u> choices and bad choices. Good things happen to us, and <u>bad</u> things happen to us. Everything that happens to us forms a little more of who we are.**

   Share an example of a good experience from your own life that has shaped you. Then say, **Tell the person to your right one good experience in your life. This can be about your family, friends, a trip, or any event so far in your life.**

   After the girls have shared, say, **We all have bad experiences, too. Some are bigger than others. Whether they're large or small, they too shape who we become. Often people feel as though God doesn't care about our hurts. "No way God has time for my little problems," we think. Not the case. Check this out.**

Specialty: Movie Clip

Show *Superman* clip (a little over an hour into the movie are a series of scenes in which Superman is saving all kinds of people and situations; in the midst of these huge problems he helps a little girl get her kitten out of a tree). After the clip say, **In the same way Superman helped the little girl, God cares about our little hurts. God's not too busy for us. We also have big hurts. God talks to us about these especially.**

Continue, **All kinds of hard, painful things happen to us. Some of them are because of choices we make. Can you think of some examples?**

After some answers *(possible answers include: friends we choose, boys we date, rebelling against our parents or teachers, etc.)* share number three.

Reality Check

3. **But most of our really major, difficult experiences have <u>nothing</u> to do with the choices we've made.**

Now say, **Some of you have had loved ones die. Some of you have loved ones with disabilities. Some of you have been in bad accidents or moved to different schools. Statistics show that at least half of you may've been hurt by divorce. Statistics say some of you may've been sexually abused, others physically abused—or verbally or emotionally. These things aren't your fault, but they totally change you forever.** (Please share a personal story that illustrates these truths.)

Continue, **The most important thing to know is, it doesn't matter what you've done or what you've said or where you were at the time—you never did anything to deserve any of these bad experiences.**

Reality Check

4. **Death, moving, divorce, accidents, and any kind of abuse all happen <u>to you</u>, not because <u>of you</u>.**

   Now instruct your girls to get into groups of three to four each and come up with an answer to question five.

Reality Check

5. **If we don't deserve these things, then why does God *allow* bad things to happen to us?**

   Have each group share answers, then add, **We must remember God loves us but often doesn't take away our pain. But God doesn't make bad things happen to punish us. So what's the deal? I'm not sure anyone can answer this question with complete confidence. However, I think we can do our best to make sense of it according to what we know about the Bible and what it tells us.**

Reality Check

6. **God hurts with us.**

   Psalm 56:8: **"You <u>keep track</u> of all my sorrows. You have collected all my tears in your bottle. You have recorded each one in your book." (NLT)**

Say, **1 Peter 5:7 says, "Turn all your worries over to him. He cares about you." (NIrV)**

Reality Check

7. **Pain isn't God's plan.**

   Revelation 21:4: "He will wipe away every tear from their eyes. There will be <u>no more</u> death or sadness. There will be no more crying or pain." (NIrV)

   Now say, **There are no tears in heaven, which means it's not God's perfect plan for us to hurt or experience sadness.**

Reality Check

8. **Isaiah 55:8 says, "'For my thoughts are not your <u>thoughts</u>, neither are your ways my <u>ways</u>,' declares the LORD."**

   Keep your eyes open to the idea that God may be doing a <u>new</u> thing.

   Continue, **God sees a big picture we can't see. Sometimes we think we know how things should work out. Then when they don't, we get really frustrated.**

   Then say, **There may be a change of plans, and if God has a better idea for my life, I think I'm in.**

   Ask, **Do you think God is interested in making us happy?** After a few girls have answered, say, **God never promised us happiness.**

   Then ask, **Do you think God is interested in our talking to him about our problems and trusting him in the midst of problems?** After a few girls have answered, say, **God always wants us to trust him, and God always wants us to talk to him. Maybe time spent with God, trusting him, can strengthen your relationship with God.**

   Then ask, **If you never struggled in life, how easy would it be to have a strong relationship with God? Would it be hard to recognize God in your day-to-day triumphs and good times?**

After some answers say, **Since God created us to have a relationship with him, it makes sense for God to allow hard, difficult things to happen sometimes—we draw closer to God through hard times. Sometimes it takes God's letting things get so bad we have no one else and nowhere else to turn so we remember God: "Hey, God's all I have left, so I guess I'll give God a shot here."**

Reality Check

9. **There is <u>hope</u>.**

   A. Romans 8:28: "And we know that in all things God works for the good of those who love him."

   B. 2 Corinthians 1:3-4: "Praise be to the God and Father of our Lord Jesus Christ, the Father of compassion and the God of all comfort, who comforts us in all our troubles, so that we can comfort those in any trouble with the comfort we ourselves receive from God."

   Say, **While hard times are often bad news, the good news is...**

Reality Check

10. **God never <u>wastes</u> a hurt.**

    Remind them, **The second reason God created us is to make the invisible God visible.** Ask, **What do you think that means?**

    After some answers say, **We need to show God's love in practical ways to others. If you've gone through something hard, God will use that for good. That's a promise!** (Please share a personal story that illustrates these truths.) Ask, **Have any of you gone through something hard and then helped someone else deal with the same problem later on? Please share with us.**

Specialty: Bible "exercise"

After your girls are done sharing their experiences of helping others, have them sit in chairs in a circle. Then read out loud the "faith hall of fame"—Hebrews 11—to the group. The chapter is only 40 verses long, so you can read quickly and with emotion. Here's the deal: With each person of faith you name, have the girls move one seat to the right if they know the person's story; those who don't stay put. (There's no true point to the activity, but it keeps the girls listening to each verse you read.)

After the game say, **All of these people went through a lot. But look how God used their lives and the pain they suffered. Billions of people have read their stories and come to know Christ because of these faith heroes.**

FORGIVING THOSE WHO'VE HURT US
Reality Check

11. **God has asked us to <u>forgive</u> as he's forgiven us. Matthew 18:21-22 says, "Then Peter came to Jesus and asked, 'Lord, how many times shall I forgive someone who sins against me? Up to seven times?' Jesus answered, 'I tell you, not seven times, but seventy-seven times.'"**

Ask your girls to close their eyes for a few minutes and think about people in their lives they haven't yet forgiven for past hurts. Tell them to take as much time as they need and to open their eyes when they're done. That's when you know it's okay to begin speaking again.

Say, **My challenge for you is to begin praying about those people and those hurts and ask God to help you forgive them. Forgiving is an important step in restoring relationships and keeping your insides whole and healthy.**

Then say, **We know God is for us. Check out these verses in Isaiah where God's talking to the Israelites while they're wandering around, questioning what in the world God's thinking:**

> **But now, this is what the LORD says—he who created you, Jacob, he who formed you, Israel: "Do not fear, for I have redeemed you; I have summoned you by name; you are mine. When you pass through the waters, I will be with you; and when you pass through the rivers, they will not sweep over you. When you walk through**

the fire, you will not be burned; the flames will not set you ablaze. For I am the LORD your God, the Holy One of Israel, your Savior." Isaiah 43:1-3

(Please share ways the latter verse has been true in your life.) Continue, **God is for you and wants to help you through stuff. And while it's okay to be upset for a while, feel sad, or even get angry, it's not okay to hold onto those feelings for extended periods. When you do, you're hurting yourself more than anyone else. Keep asking God to help you forgive and move on. You don't have to be defined by the bad things life throws at you. However...**

Reality Check

12. **If you're being abused in any way—sexually, emotionally, physically, or verbally—GET <u>HELP</u>!**

   Explain, **In those cases you need more than simply understanding that God loves you and is sad for you. Forgiving your abuser(s) will take more than patience and compassion. Other people are out there waiting to help you. They understand and know what brought them wholeness and healing. Of course you can talk to me, but you can also talk to your parents, your coach, a friend's parent, a counselor, or someone who is safe for you. They can help you find the next step in escaping abuse and moving toward forgiveness.**

TAKE OUT

Distribute **Soul Work** handouts then close in prayer, asking God to help all the girls in your group who may be hurting this week and to give them courage to forgive and seek help if they need it.

REALITY CHECK

LIVING WHOLE: DEALING WITH PAIN AND DISAPPOINTMENT

1. All the _____ in our lives shape who we are.

2. We're all surrounded by good and evil. We make _____ choices and bad choices. Good things happen to us, and _____ things happen to us. Everything that happens to us forms a little more of who we are.

3. But most of our really major, difficult experiences have _____ to do with the choices we've made.

4. Death, moving, divorce, accidents, and any kind of abuse all happen _____, not because _____.

5. If we don't deserve these things, then why does God *allow* bad things to happen to us?

6. God hurts with us.

   Psalm 56:8: "You _____ of all my sorrows. You have collected all my tears in your bottle. You have recorded each one in your book." (NLT)

7. Pain isn't God's plan.

   Revelation 21:4: "He will wipe away every tear from their eyes. There will be _____ death or sadness. There will be no more crying or pain." (NIrV)

8. Isaiah 55:8 says, "'For my thoughts are not your _____, neither are your ways my _____,' declares the LORD."

   Keep your eyes open to the idea that God may be doing a _____ thing.

9. There is _____.

   A. Romans 8:28: "And we know that in all things God works for the good of those who love him."

   B. 2 Corinthians 1:3-4: "Praise be to the God and Father of our Lord Jesus Christ, the Father of compassion and the God of all comfort, who comforts us in all our troubles, so that we can comfort those in any trouble with the comfort we ourselves receive from God."

10. God never _____ a hurt.

11. God has asked us to _____ as he's forgiven us. Matthew 18:21-22 says, "Then Peter came to Jesus and asked, 'Lord, how many times shall I forgive someone who sins against me? Up to seven times?' Jesus answered, 'I tell you, not seven times, but seventy-seven times.'"

12. If you're being abused in any way—sexually, emotionally, physically, or verbally—GET _____!

LIVING WHOLE: DEALING WITH PAIN AND DISAPPOINTMENT
Brainteasers

Are you getting good at these brainteasers? Some of them are really hard, but I bet you can get these.

1. A girl gets in a car accident and is rushed to the emergency room. Once there the doctor says, "I can't operate on her. She's my daughter." However, the doctor isn't actually the girl's dad. Why would the doctor say that?

2. Does England have a 4th of July?

3. Where was Paul going on the road to Damascus?

4. How many outs are in an inning of baseball?

5. How many animals of each species did Moses take on the ark?

Soul Work questions

1. Ask one of your heroes (someone you look up to) to tell you one event that shaped her (or him) and how God used the experience for good. Write down the answer.

2. Our life experiences include good and bad situations. Remembering that God never wastes a hurt, write down some good and bad experiences in your life. This can include your parents' divorce, abuse, a conference you went to, any big deal in your life—good or bad. You may need to come back and write things as you think of them throughout the week.

3. Once you've written one bad experience down, try to think of a way God is using, has used, or could use that hurt for good. Is there a way you could minister to other people because of the experience? Could what seems bad now actually make life better for you later? If you're dealing with abuse, use this time to pray for courage to seek help. Write down your plan of action. Who will you confide in? When? Where?

CHAPTER THREE

LIVING TRANSFORMED

INGREDIENTS

"Caution" police tape or "do not enter" tape used in crime scenes—or at least tape that looks like it (before the meeting tape off a closet door with the tape), "subject" and "statement" pieces of paper for activity, "scenarios" pieces of paper for activity, blank library cards (real or made up), two bags of microwave popcorn (one popped; one not)

REVIEW SOUL WORK

Brainteaser answers:

1. The doctor is the girl's mom
2. Yes—and a fifth, sixth, seventh...
3. Damascus
4. Six
5. Zero—Noah took the animals on the ark

APPETIZER: AMAZING GAME

Tell your girls you're going to use your amazing secret powers to send telepathic messages. Here's the trick: Pick a few people as confidants before the meeting and tell them the secret (see end of paragraph). These people could be students who won't tell the secret or other adult volunteers. After the first confidant leaves the room, have the rest of the group agree on an object for the "volunteer" to guess. Then call the person from the hallway back in; you "randomly" point to various objects in the youth room without saying a word, and your confidant indicates yes or no with her head as to whether each is the object the group picked. Repeat the feat with the next confidant. (Secret: Your confidant guesses the correct object every time because you agreed that the object you point to after any black-colored object is the correct object. Hint: Make sure there are a few black objects in the room so you don't have to point to the same black object every time.)

After the game say, **I know you're thinking what I just did with my mind is amazing. This week we're going to be talking about your mind and the amazing things you can do with it.**

QUESTIONS AND COMMENTARY

Ask, **How many of you were wondering why there's caution tape on our closet door? In fact, raise your hands—how many of you would've peeked to see what was in there if no one else were in the room?** After the girls have finished raising their hands, say, **Tons of people drive by real crime scenes just to see what's going on— why? Because we aren't supposed to know what's going on behind those taped-off areas. We aren't allowed! So we imagine what might be going on because we wonder about forbidden things— we fill in the blanks. Our minds are powerful.**

Reality Check

1. **Often as Christians we get the idea we should concentrate on _not_ sinning.**

   Ask, **What happens when we do this?** After some answers say, **All we think about is, "Don't do it. Don't do it. Don't do it." Here's the idea.** Romans 8:5 says, **"Those who live according to the sinful nature have their minds set on what that nature desires; but those who live in accordance with the Spirit have their minds set on what the Spirit desires."**

   Say, **Think of it this way: If your mind is set on what your sinful nature wants, you'll do it. But if your mind is set on what God wants, you'll do that.**

   Continue, **Another Bible translation puts it this way:**

Reality Check

2. **"Don't live under the _control_ of your sinful nature. If you do, you will think about what your sinful nature wants. Live under the control of the Holy Spirit. If you do, you will think about what the Spirit wants." (Romans 8:5, NIrV)**

3. Instead we need to <u>renew</u> our minds to the mind of Christ.

   A. Romans 12:2: "Do not conform to the pattern of this world, but be transformed by the renewing of your mind."

   Now say, **Circle the word *transformed*. Now listen to this translation of the verse from *The Message*:**

   > **"Don't become so well-adjusted to your culture that you fit into it without even thinking. Instead, fix your attention on God. You'll be changed from the inside out. Readily recognize what he wants from you, and quickly respond to it. Unlike the culture around you, always dragging you down to its level of immaturity, God brings the best out of you, develops well-formed maturity in you." (Romans 12:2)**

   Ask, **What do you think it means to "renew your mind"?**

   After some answers say, **This isn't a fancy way of saying we all need brain surgery. If you *re*bound a basketball, you get it back and get another chance to make a basket. If you *re*-up your minutes on your cell phone, you get new minutes. If you *re*build a building, you take away the old and make a new building. If you *re*new your mind, you take what you don't want and replace it with a new way of thinking.**

   Open the unpopped popcorn bag and pour out kernels. Ask, **What's wrong with this stuff?** After some answers say, **It must be transformed! A little heat then...**Now pour out the popped bag.

Reality Check

   B. Ephesians 4:23: "...be made new in the attitude of your minds."

   Say, Circle the word *new*. The words *new* and *transform* tell us what our goal is—to transform our thinking and make it new.

Reality Check

C. Colossians 3:2: "Set your minds on things above, not on earthly things."

Now say, **Circle the word** *set*. **What does it mean to set your mind on something?**

After some answers say, **It means you won't change your mind, no matter what. And what do you think happens when we set our minds on things above?**

After you get some answers, say, **If our minds are set on things above, there's little chance we'll worry about things in this life that don't matter.**

Then share number four.

Reality Check

4. **One of our biggest freedoms in life is to <u>decide what we do with our minds</u>.** (For the underlined phrase, the multiple choices listed on their sheets are A. wear panties on our heads, B. eat SPAM® until we die, and C. decide what we do with our minds.)

Go on, **You're the only one who can control what you do with your mind. But how?** (Share some examples of how we can control what we do with our minds.)

Reality Check

5. **Today's <u>thoughts</u> are tomorrow's actions.**

Explain, **You think about something enough, and you'll probably end up doing it—whether good or bad.**

Now say, **There's a phrase the church uses a lot—"the mind of Christ." What do you think the mind of Christ is like? In other words, what would Jesus** *think about*?

After some answers share number six.

Reality Check

6. The mind of <u>Christ</u> is like "...whatever is true, whatever is noble, whatever is right, whatever is pure, whatever is lovely, whatever is admirable—if anything is excellent or praiseworthy—think about such things" (Philippians 4:8).

Tell the girls, **Circle all the things you're supposed to set your mind on. What does all this mean to us? Let's examine it more closely.**

Specialty: Subject/statement game

Have all the girls stand up. Tell them to cross their arms. If a girl's left arm is on top, she's on one team; if her right arm is on top, she's on the other team. For this activity you need two girls for each round—one from each team.

The first girl will be talking about the subject you give her. She should just say or make up anything she can think of about the topic. Get the girls to pull out their best acting skills here. Shoot for the Emmy Awards. (You may want to give each girl a paper with her subject on it ahead of time to let her start thinking about the topic.)

The second girl has one phrase (written on a piece of paper and handed only to her) she needs to work into the conversation. This statement has nothing to do with the subject, yet the second girl can't just blurt it out. She can try to change the subject, but her statement has to fit in somehow. If she does it, she gets a point. If she doesn't, the other team gets a point. Set a time limit for each conversation and have the girls take turns doing each role.

*(**Leader Note:** See the **Activities** repro page; you can cut the subjects and statements into strips to give to the girls, or you can recopy them on note cards or dress them up with new fonts on your computer.)*

Subject: You know a girl who was caught smoking in the locker room after basketball practice.

Statement: I like to eat spaghetti.

Subject: Your parents are taking you to Hawaii this summer for your vacation.

Statement: My favorite color is red, but I also like purple.

Subject: You just saw the best movie last night.

Statement: One of my favorite things to do is chew ice.

Subject: My favorite hobby is boy hunting.

Statement: At 10 o'clock every night the news is on.

Subject: We're learning about transforming our minds to think as Christ does.

Statement: I love watching *American Idol*.

After the activity say, **It was hard to work these statements into the conversations. However, when you set your mind on what you needed to say, you found a way to make it work. Anything else we think about can work the same way. It's hard to think always about what is good, lovely, right, and admirable. But if we're determined to think of these things, we can. If you're determined not to gossip, you'll find a way to change the subject. If you're determined to stop thinking horrible things about someone—you can.**

Reality Check

7. **Refocus your thoughts toward positive <u>outcomes</u>.**

   Now say, **There comes a time when...**

Reality Check

8. **You must <u>choose</u> to make your feelings <u>obey</u> you. You master them.**

   Continue, **2 Corinthians 10:5 says, "We demolish arguments and every pretension that sets itself up against the knowledge of God, and we take captive every thought to make it obedient to Christ."**

   Explain, **When you fall in love, it's all you talk about and think about. When you have a big project at school or a play you're in, or you have a big solo, it's all you can focus on. You try to think about other things but you can't. Well, transforming your mind into the mind of Christ is a huge project—and it's about falling in love with him. Not many people do this hard work. But this is your life.**

   Ask, **What are some benefits of doing the hard work to renew your mind?**

Specialty: Scenarios

After you get some answers, pass out the scenarios (from Activities repro page; as with the subjects and statements, cut the scenarios into strips to give to the girls or recopy them on note cards, etc.) to four of your girls. Have the girls take turns reading the scenarios to the group.

1. When Kaylee woke up, her mom was unusually grumpy. Kaylee tried to avoid her so she wouldn't cause any trouble, but she heard her mom yelling for her as she was walking down the driveway on her way to school.

2. Britney was a nice girl with a pretty good reputation. One day she and her best friend Tami got in a fight. Tami told Britney's boyfriend Britney had cheated on him.

3. Jessica went to school, and when she got home, she noticed the money on her dresser was missing. She knew her little brother had taken the money.

4. Tina's sister had come home from a mission trip and was showing her family her pictures. In one picture, Tina noticed her sister was wearing a shirt—the same shirt Tina had been looking for all week.

After each scenario is read, ask the group two questions:

1. **What would be a normal response to this situation**? *(possible answers: anger, frustration, yelling, etc.)*

2. **If you were trying to renew your mind and have the mind of Christ, how might your response be different?**

After the activity say, **Maybe sometimes we think about how much fun it would be to sin—to do what everybody else is doing. Maybe sometimes we feel as if we're missing out because of this "Christian thing." But in reality if we could understand the joy of where we already are and know the love we have and the freedom from knowing Christ, we could fix our eyes and our thoughts on him. We could focus on Jesus and make every thought obedient to him. And we wouldn't be so focused on sinning.**

TAKE OUT

Ask your local library if you can have some blank library cards. Since the cards are computerized, the library shouldn't have a problem giving the cards away. If you can't get the library to give you some, do your best to create good fake cards to give to your whole group after the session. Give each girl a library card to help her remember to renew her mind.

Before you close, pass out the **Soul Work** handouts to your girls and close in prayer, asking God to help the girls as they make hard choices and struggle to renew their minds to make them exactly like Jesus' mind.

ACTIVITIES

SUBJECT/STATEMENT ACTIVITY

Subject: You know a girl who was caught smoking in the locker room after basketball practice.

Statement: I like to eat spaghetti.

Subject: Your parents are taking you to Hawaii this summer for your vacation.

Statement: My favorite color is red, but I also like purple.

Subject: You just saw the best movie last night.

Statement: One of my favorite things to do is chew ice.

Subject: My favorite hobby is boy hunting.

Statement: At 10 o'clock every night the news is on.

Subject: We're learning about transforming our minds to think as Christ does.

Statement: I love watching *American Idol.*

SCENARIO ACTIVITY

1. When Kaylee woke up, her mom was unusually grumpy. Kaylee tried to avoid her so she wouldn't cause any trouble, but she heard her mom yelling for her as she was walking down the driveway on her way to school.

2. Britney was a nice girl with a pretty good reputation. One day she and her best friend Tami got in a fight. Tami told Britney's boyfriend Britney had cheated on him.

3. Jessica went to school, and when she got home, she noticed the money on her dresser was missing. She knew her little brother had taken the money.

4. Tina's sister had come home from a mission trip and was showing her family her pictures. In one picture, Tina noticed her sister was wearing a shirt—the same shirt Tina had been looking for all week.

LIVING TRANSFORMED

1. Often as Christians we get the idea we should concentrate on _____ sinning.

2. "Don't live under the _____ of your sinful nature. If you do, you will think about what your sinful nature wants. Live under the control of the Holy Spirit. If you do, you will think about what the Spirit wants." (Romans 8:5, NIrV)

3. Instead we need to _____ our minds to the mind of Christ.

   A. Romans 12:2: "Do not conform to the pattern of this world, but be transformed by the renewing of your mind."

   B. Ephesians 4:23: "...be made new in the attitude of your minds."

   C. Colossians 3:2: "Set your minds on things above, not on earthly things."

4. One of our biggest freedoms in life is to _____.

   A. wear our panties on our heads.

   B. eat SPAM® until we die.

   C. decide what we do with our minds.

5. Today's _____ are tomorrow's actions.

6. The mind of _____ is like "...whatever is true, whatever is noble, whatever is right, whatever is pure, whatever is lovely, whatever is admirable—if anything is excellent or praiseworthy—think about such things" (Philippians 4:8).

7. Refocus your thoughts toward positive _____.

8. You must _____ to make your feelings _____ you. You master them.

LIVING TRANSFORMED

Brainteaser

Ready to get your brain working? This should do the trick.

Jimmy lives alone on the 11th floor of his luxurious apartment building. Each morning he leaves his room and goes to the elevator. He gets on and pushes the first-floor button. He rides all the way down, gets off, and then goes to work. Each evening after work he arrives at the building and gets on the elevator. But after work he pushes the sixth-floor button and rides to the sixth floor. He gets off and climbs the remaining five flights of stairs to the 11th floor. Every day he does the same routine—except on rainy days when he rides the elevator all the way up to the 11th floor. Why?

Soul Work questions

It's time to go get your favorite pen, a good snack, and your favorite drink. Let's get started.

1. What's a difficult situation in your life right now?

2. How has your sinful nature been controlling you in this situation? For example, have you found yourself gossiping, lying, stealing, cheating, swearing, etc., in this situation?

3. Write out the words to Philippians 4:8.

4. Your biggest freedom is what you do with your mind. How is thinking about the things you just wrote going to help you change your perspective on your hard situation?

5. In this difficult situation how can you make your thoughts obedient to you?

6. Do you find yourself more focused on what you aren't supposed to do or on what Christ thinks about?

CHAPTER FOUR

LIVING DEEPER: FRIENDS

INGREDIENTS

Copies of Friendship Prices repro page (or make up your own sheet similar to it), *Tucker: The Man and His Dream* DVD, CDs for "name that tune," *Forrest Gump* DVD, friendship bracelets (made by hand or purchased)

REVIEW SOUL WORK

Answer to the brainteaser: The man is a little person, and he can't reach past the sixth-floor elevator button—except on rainy days, when he carries an umbrella and uses it to reach the 11th-floor button.

APPETIZER: BUY A FRIEND

Prepare this game by placing dollar values on personal characteristics (use the dollar values provided on the Friendship Prices repro page or make up your own ahead of time). Tell your girls they get to buy the perfect friend, but they only have $100 each...so they need to spend wisely.

Have your girls take turns sharing which characteristics they chose and why. Then say, **What are some things missing from the list? A lot of qualities are important in a friend. We obviously want someone who loves us and cares about what's best for us. We want to enjoy doing a lot of the same things. The same sense of humor is helpful. But we sometimes overlook some other traits vital to a good friendship.**

QUESTIONS AND COMMENTARY

Say, **If I were to build an office building with 30 stories in it, I wouldn't start building on top of the ground. This wouldn't give any strength or support to the building. Or think of a tree, for example. When a seed is planted, the roots start to grow deep down. Even when the tree starts to grow above ground, the roots keep growing deeper. You can't build anything significant start-**

ing at the surface level. Real friendships work the same way. The kind of friendships that help you grow, challenge you, encourage you, and support you are the ones built on deeper than superficial or surface-level things. You need a firm foundation—deep roots. Let's find out how to become deeper.

Reality Check

1. Trust versus <u>betrayal</u>

Now say, **Honesty is one of the first things that makes a good friend. Relationships are built on trust.**

Reality Check

A. Without <u>trust</u> friendship has no foundation to grow on.

Continue, **Most people think being trustworthy basically means being able to keep a secret. That isn't all trust means, however. It's also about people being honest with each other. Telling the truth in all situations. Sometimes it's hard to be honest when someone asks those tough questions, such as, "Does this look good on me?" "Do you think Tim likes me?" "Do you think..." "What would you do if..."**

Reality Check

B. Ephesians 4:15 tells us to speak the truth in love. Proverbs 27:6 says, "Wounds from a friend can be trusted."

Next say, **Circle the words *truth* and *trusted*.**

Ask, **What do you think it means to "speak the truth with love" to one of your friends? Without using names, describe a real situation when it was hard to decide what to say.**

After some answers are shared, say, **True friends tell each other when they're wrong or messing up because true friends want the best for each other. Have you ever done that for a friend—or had a friend do the same for you? Can someone share an example without using names?**

After some sharing say, **The opposite of trustworthiness is betrayal.**

Ephesians 4:29 says, "Do not let any unwholesome talk come out of your mouths, but only what is helpful for building others up according to their needs, that it may benefit those who listen."

Explain, **Unwholesome talk isn't just swearing. It includes lies or anything negative. A friend doesn't gossip about her other friends.**

Reality Check

C. <u>Gossip</u> **is when you discuss personal things about someone behind her back.**

> **1. James 3:6 tells us that our tongue "...corrupts the whole person, sets the whole course of one's life on fire."**

> **2. Proverbs 16:28 says, "A gossip separates close friends." (NIV)**

> **3. Proverbs 11:13 says, "Gossips betray a confidence, but the trustworthy keep a secret."**

Say, **Circle** *corrupts*, *separates*, **and** *betray* **in numbers one, two, and three.**

Go on, **Honesty is always the best choice—even when it's hard. You'll end up trusted and respected. If this is a daily struggle for you, memorize Psalm 19:14: "May the words of my mouth and the meditation of my heart be pleasing in your sight, Lord, my Rock and my Redeemer."**

Reality Check

2. **Acceptance versus <u>peer pressure</u>**

A. **The best part of true, close friends is they can know who you are (if you know yourself) <u>and</u> like you <u>anyway</u>.**

Explain, **You open up to close friends, and they don't reject you. They love you for who you are and respect your differences; they're even thankful you're different from them. You complement or balance each other this way.**

Now say, **When this doesn't happen between people, the result is peer pressure.**

Reality Check

B. <u>Peer pressure</u> **isn't limited to someone trying to get you to drink, smoke, do drugs, or swear. It's also when one person expects another to be different from who God created her to be.**

Ask, **Can anyone share an example of when they've felt peer pressure?**

Specialty: Pulling Down

After some sharing tell your girls everyone needs a partner and a chair to stand on. One person stands on a chair and the other person stands on the floor. Whoever pulls her partner to where she's standing (on the floor or the chair) wins. No doubt 99 percent of the time the person on the chair will be pulled down. Then say, **It's harder to lift up than pull down. And it's always easier for someone with poor values to pull a person with good values down to her level.**

Reality Check

C. 1 Corinthians 15:33 says, "Do not be misled: 'Bad company corrupts good character.'" Proverbs 13:20 says, "Walk with the wise and become wise, for a companion of fools suffers harm."

Tell them, **Underline "bad company" and "walk with the wise and become wise."**

Now say, **While you can have non-Christian friends, these verses seem to give pretty good reasons for having best friends who're seeking Christ. Not to mention Christians are more likely to look out for you and accept how you were uniquely created and less likely to try to get you to change in**

negative ways. Though as Proverbs 4:23 warns us, "Above all else, guard your heart." No friend is perfect. Nor does going to church make people godly.

Ask, Are you accepting others for who they are? Are you someone who helps others be wise or do you corrupt people's characters? After a pause go on to point three.

Reality Check

3. **Available** versus in a clique

   Ask, **How would you feel if you called your friend up because you were crying about the bad day you just had and her response was, "Wow, you sound upset! Can I call you tomorrow—because Kim and Stacy are here right now?"**

   After some answers and discussion have them answer 3A on their **Reality Check** sheets.

Reality Check

A. Have you ever felt as if your friends' *other friends* were more important than you? Have you ever been left out?

   Ask the girls to share about what that feels like. After some discussion say, **This is really hard on a friendship. Even when someone does it unintentionally, it hurts. Some people just seem to exclude others. It's as if they feel more important with each person they reject. Cliques are never fun unless you're "in."**

Reality Check

B. Many friendships are lost because one girl joins a clique and no longer has time or room for her other "old" friends.

4. **Encouragement** versus jealousy

Read this scenario to your girls:

> **You and your friend Lisa both try out for the school musical. You're just sure this year you'll be getting the lead role. You know all the songs. You've always had small roles in the musicals and are tired of putting all that time and energy into each musical for such small roles. This is your year. The tryouts go great and you feel confident. Your friend Lisa is sure you'll get the lead, too. This is the first year she's even tried out for a musical, and she only did it because you really wanted her to. The day the parts list comes out, you and Lisa dash to the board to see what parts you'll have. At the top of the list across from the lead's name is Lisa's name. Not yours. How can that be? She didn't even care if she got a part, let alone the lead. It was your year!**

Ask, **How would you feel about Lisa getting the part?**

After some answers say, **For some reason it doesn't come naturally for us to encourage people—especially in situations where others seem to come out above us.**

Reality Check

A. **Encouragement is a character trait that takes <u>work</u> to develop. Real friends encourage each other because they're looking out for the well-being and the good of their friends.**

Explain, **Our human nature wants all the attention and credit for things. We want to be the most important person. We want our way. When these things don't happen, we become jealous.**

Now say, **To encourage someone is to want her to be the best at something, get the attention, and succeed even if you don't. This is very selfless.**

Reality Check

B. **Write out the words for Ephesians 4:29.**

5. Giving <u>versus</u> taking: "not looking to your own interests but each of you to the interests of the others" (Philippians 2:4)

Say, **Circle the word *others*. You need friends who are looking out for you, and you need to be a friend who is looking out for them.**

Specialty: Movie Clip

Show *Tucker: The Man and His Dream* clip (1:12 "What is all this cloak?" to 1:15 Abe hugs Tucker). This clip is about two friends working on making cars. When they start to get noticed, Abe decides to back out so Tucker doesn't get punished for Abe's dismal past.

After showing the clip, share point 5A.

Reality Check

A. **No friendship can be <u>one-sided.</u>**

Explain, **One person can't give all the time and the other take all the time.**

Reality Check

B. **It's <u>draining</u> for the giver, and the person taking never grows. (For the underlined word, multiple choices listed on their sheets are 1. great, 2. draining, and 3. fun.)** Share about a time when you were too needy or had a friend who only took from you...or when the balance was perfect.

Reality Check

C. **When your friend has a need, you do what you can to help; when you have a need, your friend hopefully tries to help you.**

Have the girls underline "When your friend has a need, you do what you can to help."

Reality Check

6. Listening versus knowing it all

Specialty: Name That Tune

Play a quick round of "name that tune" using snippets of popular songs from some CDs. If you're running low on time, simply say a few words from a song and let the students finish the sentence or lyric.

Then say, **We spend a lot of time listening to music. We can repeat most of the lyrics of most of the songs we listen to. But are we listening well to our friends? Now share point 6A.**

Reality Check

A. James 1:19 says, "Everyone should be <u>quick</u> to listen, <u>slow</u> to speak and slow to become angry."

Continue, **Do you spend more time listening to your friends and accepting their ideas, doing things they express interest in, and letting them have a place to vent—or do you worry about what you want to say and do and always have to tell the funniest story? Think about that for a moment.**

Pause for a short time (30 seconds or so). Then say, **Have you ever had a friend who knew everything? When you told a story, she had a better story. When you had an accomplishment, she had accomplished more. When you needed to vent, let out your feelings, she said she knew just what you had to do to fix the problem. She was full of advice and never thought she was wrong.**

Reality Check

B. The first sign of wisdom is knowing you don't know it <u>all</u>. Take time to listen.

Say, **Often listening is all you want from someone. Often it's all people want from you.**

Reality Check

7. Forgiving versus holding <u>grudges</u>

> **A. In every friendship (and family) people are going to make mistakes. *You're* going to make <u>mistakes</u>.**

Say, **It's inevitable. But you have a choice to forgive and move on or to hold a grudge and destroy a relationship.**

Reality Check

> **B. Ephesians 4:32 says, "Be kind and compassionate to one another, forgiving each other, just as in Christ God forgave you."**

Tell the girls to underline "God forgave you."

Specialty: Piggyback Challenge

Have everyone pick a partner. One needs to get on the other's back piggyback style. Have all the pairs walk in a circle around the room. When a team gets tired, they sit down. The last team standing wins.

After the activity say, **Grudges feel this way. We can carry them for a while, but after a long time they get too heavy and we can't keep going.**

Reality Check

> **C. Forgiveness is more for <u>me</u> than for the person being forgiven.** (For the underlined word, multiple choices listed on their sheets are 1. Mom, 2. God, and 3. me.)

Next say, **Here's what a friendship looks like when the relationship is good.**

Specialty: Movie Clip

Show *Forrest Gump* clip (chapter 18 "It's funny how you remember..." to chapter 20 "Jenny and me was like peas and carrots"). Use this clip to show how great friendships can be if they're more than superficial. Forrest feels accepted for who he is. Jenny has to put up with a lot of ridicule for being his friend, but she always feels she has someone out there who loves her no matter what she's going through.

After the clip ask, **Do you think Forrest and Jenny have a good friendship? Why or why not?** After some answers and discussion say, **We need friends. God knew Adam needed someone so he wouldn't be alone, so God gave Adam Eve. God made us in a way so we need relationships.**

Continue, **Some of you don't have friends who are good for you and encourage you in your relationship with Christ. Pray for God to send you a good friend. God will. Keep your eyes open for God's answer to that prayer; it isn't always the answer you think it may be.**

Now say, **Others of you aren't being the friends you need to be. God can give you the strength to become a better friend. Often when you become a stronger, more encouraging person, the same kind of people will want to be friends with you.**

Finally, say, **A good way to see what kind of friend you are is to look at the friends you have. Do they have a reputation for being kind, loving, and accepting? Or is their reputation more in line with being mean, rude, disrespectful, and unaccepting? Whatever their reputation is, yours probably is, too. We're usually like the people we hang around—remember? The good news is, it's never too late to change for the better. In your Soul Work you'll get a chance to examine what kind of friend you really are.**

TAKE OUT

Before you end the meeting, give everyone a friendship bracelet and challenge the girls to wear the bracelets all week to remind them to be good friends. You can do this in several ways:

▷ You can make the bracelets yourself by braiding them or getting fancy with knots.

▷ You can go buy some cheap ones.

▷ You can ask a couple of the girls in your group to make them the week prior to the lesson as a ministry—you may want to call them midweek to be sure they're doing it.

▷ You can make the bracelets during class—just braid quickly.

▷ You can add it to their **Soul Work**, assuming everyone knows how to make friendship bracelets.

Give everyone a copy of this week's **Soul Work** and close in prayer.

FRIENDSHIP PRICES

You get to buy the perfect friend, but you only have $100...so spend wisely! Circle your choices.

$16 athletic	$16 intelligent	$8 has a cute brother
$20 sense of humor	$20 sincere	$12 loyal
$12 popular	$12 Christian	$14 forgiving
$20 has a car	$20 honest	$10 available
$12 reliable	$8 same age	$10 encouraging
$12 similar interests	$8 good-looking	$14 selfless
$16 good listener	$16 wealthy	
$20 fun	$8 accepting	
	$8 nice parents	
	$12 doesn't gossip	

From *Living as a Young Woman of God* by Jen Rawson. Permission to reproduce this page granted only for use in buyer's youth group.
Copyright ©2008 by Youth Specialties

REALITY CHECK

LIVING DEEPER: FRIENDS

1. Trust versus _____

    A. Without _____ friendship has no foundation to grow on.

    B. Ephesians 4:15 tells us to speak the truth in love. Proverbs 27:6 says, "Wounds from a friend can be trusted."

    C. _____ is when you discuss personal things about someone behind her back.

        1. James 3:6 tells us that our tongue "...corrupts the whole person, sets the whole course of one's life on fire."

        2. Proverbs 16:28 says, "A gossip separates close friends." (NIV)

        3. Proverbs 11:13 says, "Gossips betray a confidence, but the trustworthy keep a secret."

2. Acceptance versus _____

    A. The best part of true, close friends is they can know who you are (if you know yourself) _____ like you _____.

    B. _____ isn't limited to someone trying to get you to drink, smoke, do drugs, or swear. It's also when one person expects another to be different from who God created her to be.

    C. 1 Corinthians 15:33 says, "Do not be misled: 'Bad company corrupts good character.'" Proverbs 13:20 says, "Walk with the wise and become wise, for a companion of fools suffers harm."

3. _____ versus in a clique

    A. Have you ever felt as if your friends' *other friends* were more important than you? Have you ever been left out?

    B. Many friendships are _____ because one girl joins a clique and no longer has time or room for her other "old" friends.

4. _____ versus jealousy

    A. Encouragement is a character trait that takes _____ to develop. Real friends encourage each other because they're looking out for the well-being and the good of their friends.

    B. Write out the words for Ephesians 4:29.

5. Giving _____ taking: "not looking to your own interests but each of you to the interests of the others" (Philippians 2:4)

    A. No friendship can be _____.

    B. It's _____ for the giver and the person taking never grows.

        1. great

        2. draining

        3. fun

    C. When your friend has a need, you do what you can to help; when you have a need, your friend hopefully tries to help you.

6. _____ versus knowing it all

    A. James 1:19 says, "Everyone should be _____ to listen, _____ to speak and slow to become angry."

    B. The first sign of wisdom is knowing you don't know it _____. Take time to listen.

7. Forgiving versus holding _____

    A. In every friendship (and family) people are going to make mistakes. *You're* going to make _____.

    B. Ephesians 4:32 says, "Be kind and compassionate to one another, forgiving each other, just as in Christ God forgave you."

    C. Forgiveness is more for _____ than for the person being forgiven.

        1. Mom

        2. God

        3. me

LIVING DEEPER: FRIENDS

Brainteasers

Let's see how your brains are working this week.

1. Divide 30 by one half and add 10. What's the answer? _____

2. I have in my hand two U.S. coins that total 55 cents in value. One isn't a nickel. What are the two coins? _____

3. Take two apples from three trees, and what do you have? _____

4. Is it legal in North Carolina for a man to marry his widow's sister? _____ Why? _____

5. A man builds a house with four sides, and it's rectangular in shape. Each side has a southern exposure. A big bear comes wandering by. What color is the bear? _____

Soul Work questions

Oh, you are sooooo good! Take a quick breather from that serious thinking and let's get serious about becoming a friend worth keeping.

1. What are some of the character traits you love about your friends?

2. Ask your mom what her favorite qualities in a friend are. List them here.

3. Are you wearing your bracelet every day? Has it helped remind you to make good choices about friendships?

4. Call your best friend. Really. (If you're grounded from the phone, this will cause a serious problem. It sounds as if you may need a lesson on families.) You're going to interview your very best friend. These are some tough questions—be ready for some real answers.

   A. How do I do at being honest and not gossiping?

   B. Do you feel accepted by me
      1. all of the time
      2. some of the time
      3. not much of the time

   C. Do you feel as if I let you be who you want to—I don't ask you to change?

   D. Have you ever felt as if I didn't have time for you?

   E. Do I encourage others to do and be the best they can, or do I worry more about looking better than others?

F. How well do I meet your needs as a friend?

G. Would you say I'm quick to listen or quick to speak?

H. Is there anything I'm holding over your head as a grudge that you wish I'd get over?

I. Is there anything stupid I've done and never tried to set right with you?

CHAPTER FIVE

LIVING PRAISEWORTHY: FAMILY

INGREDIENTS

Fake medals/medallions on neck lanyards (you can get them at a party store or in the party section of a large retail store)

OPTIONAL PARENT LETTER

You may want to send the letter (found in the repro section after this session's text) to parents to encourage them in their roles. Make sure you do so well in advance of this week's meeting.

REVIEW THE SOUL WORK

Answers to the brainteasers:

1. 70.

2. A half-dollar and a nickel—one isn't a nickel but the other is.

3. Two apples.

4. No, he's dead.

5. White—the house is on the North Pole (that's how it can have four sides facing south), so the only bears are polar bears.

APPETIZER

"Family Feud": This is somewhat like the TV game show. You need two teams. Teams try to guess the top five (or three if you want to save time) answers to a question. To determine who goes first, you need one representative from each team for a face-off challenge. You ask the question, and the first player to get a right answer determines the team that goes first. Each team takes turns guessing. They get points according to the value of the answers they give. The number-one answer is worth 500 points, number two is worth 400, number three is worth 300, number four is worth 200, and number five is worth 100. (Just as a reminder: In the TV game they play three rounds in a half-hour so you don't have to do all these. Just use your favorites and move on—this isn't your entire session!)

Question: What's the most popular comfort food?

1. chocolate

2. ice cream

3. pizza

4. candy

5. chicken noodle soup

Question: What floats on water?

1. boat

2. raft

3. plants/flowers

4. people

5. wood

Question: What's the most popular chocolate treat?

1. SNICKERS®

2. Reese's®

3. Kit Kat®

4. Butterfinger®

5. Milky Way®

Question: What do people use computers for?

1. research

2. work

3. school

4. entertainment

5. e-mail

Question: What's the most common household pet?

1. cat

2. dog

3. fish

4. hamster

5. bird

Question: What's something all little kids hate?

1. veggies

2. bedtime

3. shots

4. the dentist

5. bullies

QUESTIONS AND COMMENTARY

After the game ask, **What would happen if we had no street lights or stop signs? What purpose do they serve?**

After you get some responses, say, **They're a pain when you're in a hurry or when you catch all the red lights. However, when the light is green or you're at an intersection with no stop sign, you can be confident you don't have to stop.**

Now ask, **What's the purpose of the president? What's the purpose of school principals?**

After some discussion say, **Romans 13:1-2 tells us—**

> **Let everyone be subject to the governing authorities, for there is no authority except that which God has established. The authorities that exist have been established by God. Consequently, whoever rebels against the authority is rebelling against what God has instituted, and those who do so will bring judgment on themselves.**

Continue, **Everyone has someone to answer to—even Jesus! The Bible tells us he was obedient to God unto death. This verse tells us God established the idea of authorities.**

Ask, **Was this a good idea? Why do we have authorities and rules?**

After some answers and discussion, ask, **Who do you have to answer to?**

After some answers ask, **Which of your authority figures is the most important one? If some of your girls reply "parents," say, Even though parents are very important to listen to, God is your ultimate authority. So do you know what God says about your authorities? Listen to Ephesians 6:1-3: "Children obey your parents in the Lord, for this is right. 'Honor your father and mother'— which is the first commandment with a promise—'so that it may go well with you and that you may enjoy long life on the earth.'"**

Then say, **Honor and obey? You had to know this was coming. Don't be mad at me—I didn't write this stuff! God put your parents next in charge after himself. 2 John 1:6 says, "And this is love: that we walk in obedience to his commands." So when we honor and obey our parents, we're actually showing love and respect to God.**

Say, **Getting along with your family can be really hard, mostly because you're around each other so much and also because you know how to push each others' buttons. Some family situations can be extra tough if they involve divorce, stepparents, or foster parents. However, our parents, with the exception of abusive parents, are really trying their best to help us. They've lived awhile and would love to save you from learning some lessons the hard way.**

Reality Check

1. My parents are often the only ones <u>looking out</u> for me.

Now say, **We often take our parents' care and concern for us and return it with a bad attitude, disobedience, and disrespect. None of your parents are perfect, but most of them are really trying to do the best job they can. If you take a step back, you have to know your parents—to the best of their ability—make their decisions based on the idea that** you're the most precious person on earth and they want what's best for you. You may not agree with their choices, but I think we could all agree most parents want what's best for their kids. You can't pick who you have as your family. You're stuck. So you may as well figure out how to make the next few years go as smoothly as possible.

Then say, **And I'm here to help. I'm going to let you in on four secret rules to revolutionize your life. If you live by these ideas, your relationship with your parents will be much healthier, and you'll probably end up with more freedom— and respect. The key is not to worry about changing your parents. You can only change yourself. However, when you take care of changing yourself, I bet you'll be amazed at what you see happening with your parents.**

Reality Check

2. **Rule number one: Act like an adult.**

   Explain, **This doesn't mean move out and get a job. It means handling the freedoms and privileges of adulthood.**

   Colossians 3:22-23 says, "...obey your earthly masters in everything; and do it, not only when their eye is on you and to curry [win] their favor, but with sincerity of heart and reverence for the Lord. Whatever you do, work at it with all your heart, as working for the Lord."

   Say, **Underline "not only" and "working for the Lord" on your Reality Check sheets.** Then ask, **How do you think this verse applies to your relationship with your parents?**

   After some answers say, **If you're acting like an adult, and you're working for the Lord, you would handle things on your own because that's what adults do. How would this change your attitude about things like homework, cleaning your room, and how you talk to your parents?**

Reality Check

3. **Rule numero two: Find out what small things matter a ton to your parents—then do those things.**

Next say, **This is where the whole "obey" thing comes in. What are some small things in your day-to-day life your parents are always asking you to do?**

After some answers say, **You'll gain their respect—and gain more freedom—when you start doing these things without being asked. When your parents tell you to take out the trash, you know eventually they'll make you do it. What about cleaning your room? Or doing your homework? So skip their nagging and just do the task right away.**

Philippians 2:14 says, "Do everything without grumbling or arguing."

Tell the girls to underline the word *everything*.

Reality Check

4. **The third rule: Stay away from your parents' anger so you are <u>praiseworthy</u>. Romans 13:3 says, "If you do what is right, you won't need to be afraid of your rulers. But watch out if you do what is wrong! You don't want to be afraid of those in authority, do you? Then do what is right. The one in authority will praise you." (NIrV)**

Have the girls underline the words *afraid* and *praise*.

Then say, **This rule is pretty significant. It holds a key that could unlock your happiness while you're living at home. Because when you do right, what do you think your parents will do? They'll praise you. Your whole goal is to make it easy for them to say yes when you ask them for something. When you follow these three rules and act praiseworthy, your parents find it much easier to say yes and give you more freedom.**

Reality Check

5. **Rule number four: Let your parents be <u>in charge</u>.**

   Say, **They are, after all, your parents—and sometimes it's easy to forget who's in charge, especially if they've given you many freedoms. Let them be and feel like the parents.**

Exodus 20:12 says, "Honor your father and your mother, so that you may live long in the land the LORD your God is giving you."

Have the girls underline the word *honor*.

Reality Check

6. <u>Honor</u> means: "great respect given because of worth, to have or show great respect for."

Now explain, **This means not just giving respect when you feel your parents deserve it, but showing it even when you don't think they deserve it or you don't feel like giving it.**

Then say, **Let's check out how life can be when you follow these four rules.**

Specialty: Scenario

Have your girls follow along as you read the scenario and the four rules/questions as they've been applied to the scenario. Have your girls shout out answers.

Read, **Scenario: Your parents have given you a 10 p.m. curfew on Friday nights. But you really want to extend the curfew to 10:30 or even—gasp—11 p.m. Now we'll go through the four rules to revolutionize your life.**

Rule one: What are ways to act like an adult to help you get the curfew extended? *(possible answers: be home on time for the current curfew; get schoolwork done on time; be grateful for staying out late; wake up Mom to say I'm home safe when I come in on time; if I'm late, don't make excuses and don't wake up the next day in a bad mood; help my parents decide on a consequence for being late or offer a trial period of coming home later or earlier; respect their "no")*

Rule two: What small things matter to your parents that are keeping you from having a later curfew?

Rule three: How can you stay out of your parents' anger and be praiseworthy?

Rule four: Did you assume they'd change your curfew to 11 p.m. because you forgot they're in charge? How could you show them they're in charge?

Create three groups from your large group by having everyone play rock-paper-scissors to divide the groups—all the rocks in one group, papers in another, and scissors in the third. Then have the small groups discuss the four scenarios in question seven, fill in the answers on their **Reality Check** sheets, then share their answers with the entire group. (You can offer help by prompting them with possible answers if they get stuck.)

Reality Check

7. **With your group use your handy-dandy rules to reply to the following scenarios (A, B, C, and D).**

   Rule 1: What are some ways you can act like an adult to help the situation?

   Rule 2: What small things matter to your parents that you could do to get the result you want in the scenario?

   Rule 3: How can you stay out of your parents' anger and be praise-worthy in the situation?

   Rule 4: How can you let your parents be the ones in charge and be respectful of them in this case?

   Scenario A. You want more freedom to go places when you want.

   (possible answers: make sure my parents know what I'm doing and who I'm with; make wise choices about where I spend my time if I'm not being responsible with my time and where I'm going now—more freedom means more trouble, and my parents care about who I'm spending my time with.)

   Scenario B. You want some money to go do something.

   (possible answers: don't keep my parents' change, bring them a receipt, say thanks, and offer to work for the money.)

Scenario C. You want to redecorate your room to look more like a teenager's room.

(possible answers: keep my room clean now; do little things without spending money to make the room look better; sit down with my parents and ask how they'd like to see the room looking but also express my ideas.)

Scenario D. You want to start babysitting for a little extra cash.

(possible answers: show how responsible I can be taking care of the family pet—if I can't feed a pet, why would I be trusted to feed a kid? Make lunch on a Saturday to show I can cook. Look into taking a babysitting course; ask how my curfew would relate to a babysitting situation and whether my parents would have any special guidelines. Be loving to my own siblings—you know, those kids who are already in my life.)

A quick look at siblings

Say, **Someone describe your relationships with your brothers and/ or sisters for us.**

After you receive some descriptions, ask, **Have you ever heard this phrase?** and share number eight.

Reality Check

8. **The people we <u>love</u> the most are the people we <u>hurt</u> the most.**

   Then ask your girls to volunteer to share a little bit about fighting with their siblings. After you've heard a few descriptions, say, **Those descriptions are very common. But why do we think we have the right to treat our siblings so poorly? We'll do anything to keep our friends, but when it comes to a brother or sister—who cares?**

   After you've heard some answers, say, **Our sisters and brothers can't stop being around us. Even if they stay in their rooms most of the time, eventually, they get hungry and come out, and we're forced to be around them. One of our biggest fears is being rejected completely. Our siblings can't com-**

pletely reject us because they're part of our families, so we feel as though we've found the perfect people to take out our frustrations on. But remember...

Reality Check

9. You're a <u>role model</u> for your siblings.

   Now say, **Obviously, younger siblings look up to you. But even when you are the younger sibling, the Bible tells us you can be someone others look up to.**

   1 Timothy 4:12 says, "Don't let anyone look down on you because you are young, but set an example...in speech, in conduct, in love, in faith and in purity."

   Say, **Underline "set an example."**

   Then go on, **Besides, you're on the same team—you should have a special camaraderie—a spirit of friendly fellowship—with your siblings. You're in this together and you're in it for the long haul. If you treated your siblings as you do your friends or even better, what would happen?**

   After some answers say, **When you act praiseworthy, your parents will trust you more and have fewer reasons to get upset with you. You'll find real freedom in this. You and your parents and siblings will enjoy each other a lot more.**

   Next say, **Check out this verse.**

Reality Check

10. **"Do nothing out of selfish ambition or vain conceit. Rather, in humility value others above yourselves, not looking to your own interests but each of you to the interests of the <u>others</u>." (Philippians 2:3-4)**

    Continue, **Are you doing this at home? The verse doesn't say anyone is better than you or more important than you. God made each of us. So God simply wants us to treat others with the most respect and love we have. Are you showing God's glory, making the invisible God visible, to your family? Are you loving them with the mind of Christ? Are you devoted to being the best sister and daughter you can?**

TAKE OUT

Pass out those fake medals, one to each girl. Then say, **When your parents compliment you and are proud of you, it's as if they give you a gold medal for your behavior. If they're proud of your actions and feel you're acting responsibly and showing that you're worthy of being treated as an adult, they'll be a lot easier to live with—and so will you! Use this medal to remind you of how you need to treat your parents. And remember our little keys, our rules, to improving your relationship with your family.**

Distribute the **Soul Work** handouts for the week and then close in prayer.

OPTIONAL PARENT LETTER

Dear [insert parents' names here],

I thought I'd give you a peek into what we're doing. We've been talking about some of the important relationships in our lives. This week we're talking about YOU. The good news is, I'm on your side—I'm on your girls' sides, too! My hope is together we can all make life at home a little easier.

When we read the Bible, we meet all the great people who've done incredible things. But look at this verse: "By faith Moses' parents hid him for three months after he was born, because they saw he was no ordinary child, and they were not afraid of the king's edict" (Hebrews 11:23). In the "Faith Hall of Fame" chapter, parents are specifically mentioned. I love that. Only because of his parents' openness and obedience to God could Moses go on and become what he was. Their bravery and courage saved him. They saw he was special even as a newborn baby. I know you can see the potential in your daughters. I can see it, too.

As you're probably noticing, the hardest relationship teenage girls usually have is with their moms. A teenage daughter can see her mother as the hurdle to her autonomy. She's working so hard to become independent, and sometimes she sees your protection and love as barriers to her independence. This is where the adage of "You're her parent, not her best friend" is so true. Stay strong and stand your ground. Once a daughter grows up, she's usually closest to her mom. I'm trying hard to involve you in the weekly Soul Work the girls are doing to keep those lines of communication open.

Dads are vital, too. Studies show girls who have emotionally involved dads are better adjusted to life all around. Obviously, you probably have to work, but when you're home, paying attention to your daughters (and your sons) is vital to their emotional well-being. You need to keep track and be sure you hug your kids at least once a day. Their futures really do depend on your availability.

Working with you,

LIVING PRAISEWORTHY: FAMILY

1. My parents are often the only ones _____ for me.

2. Rule number one: _____ like an adult.

   Colossians 3:22-23 says, "...obey your earthly masters in everything; and do it, not only when their eye is on you and to curry [win] their favor, but with sincerity of heart and reverence for the Lord. Whatever you do, work at it with all your heart, as working for the Lord."

3. Rule numero two: Find out what _____ things matter a ton to your parents—then do those things.

   Philippians 2:14 says, "Do everything without grumbling or arguing."

4. The third rule: Stay away from your parents' anger so you are _____.

   Romans 13:3 says, "If you do what is right, you won't need to be afraid of your rulers. But watch out if you do what is wrong! You don't want to be afraid of those in authority, do you? Then do what is right. The one in authority will praise you." (NIrV)

5. Rule number four: Let your parents be _____.

   Exodus 20:12 says, "Honor your father and your mother, so that you may live long in the land the LORD your God is giving you."

6. _____ means: "great respect given because of worth, to have or show great respect for."

7. With your group use your handy-dandy rules to reply to the following scenarios (A, B, C, and D).

   Rule 1: What are some ways you can act like an adult to help the situation?

Rule 2: What small things matter to your parents that you could do to get the result you want in the scenario?

Rule 3: How can you stay out of your parents' anger and be praiseworthy in the situation?

Rule 4: How can you let your parents be the ones in charge and be respectful of them in this case?

Scenario A. You want more freedom to go places when you want.

Scenario B. You want some money to go do something.

Scenario C. You want to redecorate your room to look more like a teenager's room.

Scenario D. You want to start babysitting for a little extra cash.

A quick look at siblings

8. The people we _____ the most are the people we _____
   the most.

9. You're a _____ for your siblings.

   1 Timothy 4:12 says, "Don't let anyone look down on you because you are young, but
   set an example...in speech, in conduct, in love, in faith and in purity."

10. "Do nothing out of selfish ambition or vain conceit. Rather, in humility value others
    above yourselves, not looking to your own interests but each of you to the interests of
    the _____." (Philippians 2:3-4)

SOUL WORK

LIVING PRAISEWORTHY: FAMILY
Brainteasers

We talked about family this week, so go ask your family to help you out with these.

1. diff erence _____

2. take take _____

3. ban ana _____

4. options options options options _____

5. O, 144 _____

Soul Work questions

1. How does God tell us to act toward our parents?

2. 1 Corinthians 13 is considered the "love chapter" of the Bible. I want you to rewrite verses 4-7, only instead of writing the word love where it appears in the Bible, I want you to write your name.

3. How are you fulfilling these standards for love as a daughter and/or sister? (If you can do these things, they'll help you be praiseworthy.)

4. Write down one way you can serve and love each family member this week. (And then don't forget to do each item, too!)

5. Write about one example this week when you tried to act like an adult or made a small thing into a big thing to honor your parents. Did your parents seem to notice?

CHAPTER SIX

LIVING COMPLETE: BOYS AND THE SEARCH FOR TRUE LOVE

INGREDIENTS

The List handout (one copy per girl), magazines, glue, scissors, paper, a few simple 24-piece puzzles of princesses, *The Missing Piece Meets the Big O* by Shel Silverstein, *Can't Hardly Wait* DVD, another puzzle you can use to write verses on the backs of the pieces (one piece per girl)

Leader Note: *This chapter is a bit longer than the others in this book, so you'll either want to prepare more time for this session than usual or pick and choose which activities to cover so you can fit the session into your allotted study time.*

REVIEW SOUL WORK

Here are those ringy-dingy brainteaser answers:

1. Splitting the difference
2. Double take
3. Banana split
4. Several options
5. Oh, gross!

APPETIZER

Hand out copies of **The List**, magazines, glue, scissors, and paper. Tell your group, **We're going to see who can find a man, plan a date, and top off the perfect night fastest. You're on a mission to plan the perfect evening for the perfect man—who you'll also need to find. You're in a race to find the items on your list in magazines. Each item is vital in planning this ideal night. Once you've found an item, cut it out and glue it to your paper. You don't need to go in order. Whoever finds all the items for her supreme date first wins.**

After the game tell your best story of love (or lack of love!) from middle school. Students devour this stuff. They can't imagine you in their shoes, but telling the story helps them see that you're just like them and can be trusted with their hurts, joys, and life issues. Even a sad story of being dumped means you've been in their shoes and you get it.

After you share your story, say, **We all want to be loved and accepted. Some of you have had several boyfriends and others haven't had one yet. Middle school is often the time when all of this starts to become such a huge deal. Whether you have a boyfriend or not doesn't change that you're starting to notice those boys—even those of you who won't admit it.**

QUESTIONS AND COMMENTARY

Ask, **What's so wonderful about boys?** After some answers ask, **What do you hate about boys?**

After some answers continue, **We all get dressed up to go to school, the mall, and dances to look our best. Why? Why do we care what boys think about us?**

Then say, **Those of you who've had a boyfriend and gotten dumped know that stinks. How can something so wonderful be so sad and make us feel so lonely? Yet we still want another guy to like us even when we know it can hurt so much.**

Go on, **Then during times such as around Valentine's Day a lot of girls and guys end up feeling worse about themselves because no one sent them Valentine wishes. So this guy/girl thing that's supposed to be so great makes us feel so bad. How can that be?**

Now say, **You can get really confused trying to know how you feel and what you think, let alone what boys are thinking and feeling. Then when you throw in the fact that our culture doesn't tell you the truth about boys and relationships, it muddies up the waters even more. Sometimes you may be embarrassed by some of the feelings you're having, which is normal, too. Teenagers write anonymous letters to youth magazines all the time asking all kinds of questions because the kids don't want to ask those questions of people they know. Then everyone else reads the letters and answers because they're so thankful someone asked the questions they were too embarrassed to ask. Obviously, you have a lot of confusion and feelings going on. You feel these things because...**

Reality Check

1. **<u>God</u> placed those <u>desires</u> in you.**

   Say, **God gave you these feelings and desires for good reasons. You simply need to understand what you're dealing with.**

   Ask, **Since these feelings can be so strong in both good and bad ways, why do you think God would place these feelings and desires in you?**

   After some responses share point two.

Reality Check

2. **If no women wanted to be loved by men (and vice versa), no one would get <u>married</u> and no one would have <u>kids</u>—and then no one would be left on earth.**

   Explain, **Marriage was God's idea. God's happy we can marry, love, and share the rest of our lives with a spouse. Marriage is part of God's plan for those of us who get married. And God loves those who don't get married just as much and has just as many plans for them.**

Specialty: Puzzle Fun

Split the girls into teams of no more than four each. Set each princess puzzle box in a different area of the youth room. Depending on your group's size, you can set this game up two ways. For larger groups (teams of more than three girls): When a team finishes one puzzle, the team needs to take it apart and put all the pieces back in the box. Have the teams go around the room trying to complete all the puzzles. The team to finish all the puzzles first wins. Have each team leave the last completed puzzle put together. Smaller group (teams of three or less): Have each team do only one puzzle and leave it put together when done. The first team done wins.

Here's the trick. One puzzle needs to have one piece missing—preferably a piece from the middle. Play it off as if you didn't know. Maybe take a second to look in the box and on the floor, then say, **That's what I get for getting puzzles at a garage sale!** Then enthusiastically tell them to skip it and keep going.

After the game concludes, say, **We each have a hole in us. An emptiness or loneliness—as if something is missing, the same as this puzzle** (indicating the puzzle with a piece missing). **Only one piece can fill in the spot to complete it.** Pick up a couple of pieces from the other puzzles and say, **I can try other pieces and other shapes, but only one will work.**

Go on, **You can try to fill the feeling of emptiness or loneliness with boys—or money, stuff, jobs, sports, good grades, music, anything really—but they won't fit. Just as with the puzzle pieces, they may cover up the hole, but the hole is still there.**

Reality Check

3. You're not looking for a boyfriend—you're seeking <u>true love</u>.

Specialty: "True Love" Test

This is just a silly way to start talking to the girls about true love. Here's my example. My maiden name was Jennifer Dawn Harris; my husband's name is Kenneth River Rawson. Now look for all the letters from our names in TRUE and LOVE and then line them up as a math equation this way:

T—1

L—0

R—6

O—1

U—0

V—1

E—5

E—5

12

7

Put the two numbers next to each other and add a percent sign, and you get 127 percent (127%).

Say, **Let me show you the "true love" test. For each letter in my name and the name of the guy I like—in my case, my husband—that matches the letters in TRUE LOVE, I get one point.** Then show the girls on a whiteboard or poster how your own example works out.

Now say something like this, tailoring the numbers or celebrities to fit with your own example: **So if I'd done this when I first met my husband, naturally I'd have known we could get married, and it would all work out and we'd live happily ever after. It's a good thing I married him then—because if he'd have just sat down to do the same with Drew Barrymore, he'd have seen that their true love was 138 percent, and then where would I be? Not happily ever after! Or I might've been stuck with Elvis Aaron Presley at a mere 98 percent. Who could be truly happy with only 98-percent true love? Close call.** Let the girls try their own examples with guys they like for fun for a minute. Then ask, **But is this really how to figure out what makes true love?**

Reality Check

4. 1 Corinthians 13 is the love chapter in the Bible. Verses 4-7 list things that show true love: Love is <u>patient</u>, kind, does not envy, does not boast, it is not proud, it does not dishonor others, it is not <u>self-seeking</u>, it is not easily angered, it keeps no record of wrong, does not delight in evil but rejoices with truth, always <u>protects</u>, trusts, hopes, and perseveres.

   Then ask, **Do you know a man who can live up to all that?** Share number 5.

Reality Check

5. Only God can <u>meet</u> these desires.

   Now say, **Have you ever heard the question "Is there anything God can't do?" What do you think? Actually, we do know that answer. God can't lie. God can't sin. And it's impossible for God not to love. 1 John 4:8 tells us God is love! It doesn't say God knows how to love—God _is_ love. God's love never fails.**

All those things in 1 Corinthians 13 will always be true all the time about God, no matter what, because God is those things. Boys can love us the best they know how, but...

Reality Check

6. God <u>is</u> love.

   Continue, **God designed us so we'd keep seeking to be filled until we find God. We can try to fill our lives with what the world has to offer, but those things will never fulfill us. Our puzzle will never be complete until we allow God into our lives and trust him for our value, worth, and acceptance.**

Reality Check

7. Matthew 22:37 says, "'Love the Lord your God with all your <u>heart</u> and with all your <u>soul</u> and with all your <u>mind</u>.'"

   Next say, **If you love God with all your heart, all your soul, and all your mind, what's left? In other words, if you're loving God with all of your emotions—heart, all of your character—soul, and all of your thoughts—mind, then what part of you isn't loving God? What part of you is left seeking to be filled? What's left? Nothing. You've found your value, acceptance, and worth in God.**

   Then say, **The problem is we don't always do this. We forget God can fill all those needs. We forget God is love and only God has the missing piece we're looking for.**

Reality Check

8. God placed those feelings and desires in you to help you keep <u>seeking</u> God.

   Take out the missing piece of the puzzle you hid and place it in the incomplete puzzle. Then say, **So does this mean it's wrong to date boys, to have a boyfriend and want his attention, since we should be seeking God?** *(One possible answer is along the lines of: When Christ is at the center of who we are and we let him be all we need, then and only then can boys play a proper role in our lives.)*

Leader Note: *This is a great time for discussion, so let your girls go for it until they've said their piece.*

Specialty: Illustration (Optional)

After the discussion it's time for you to illustrate your point. With middle school girls you may've already found some illustrations can go great and others can bomb. Some girls have started thinking abstractly and others haven't. So hang in there and don't give up. If they don't get it, that's all right. They'll still connect with at least one point in this lesson they can take home.

By far my favorite way to illustrate this point is by using *The Missing Piece Meets the Big O* by Shel Silverstein. It's an excellent book. You can check it out at the library. The only problem is you'll need to do some groundwork before and after to help the girls connect. However, it's worth it if you help the girls understand the point. Otherwise, you can always use one of the examples given later.

Before you read, be sure to point out that each girl is the missing piece. When you and I read this story, we like to see the story unfold and relate to it as we go, then get the whole point at the end. But middle school girls may need to skip the element of surprise and be clued in from the get-go on who they are if they're going to get the full effect of the story for the point you want to make. Also, be sure to let the girls know this is about the attempt to complete themselves with boys. You can say something like this: **You may think you'll be happier with a boyfriend. You think you'll feel prettier and more lovable and be more valuable. It's as if you're missing something—you feel you're not complete without a boyfriend. Because of this, you may go to great lengths to have a boyfriend. Look what happens to the missing piece in this story on its search.**

Read *The Missing Piece Meets the Big O.*

Debrief questions—

▷ **What are some of the things the missing piece tries to do that don't work?**

▷ **At one point it finds an "O" it fits into nicely, but what happens?**

▷ **It runs into the Big O at one point, but that doesn't work out either—why?**

▷ **What happens to make the missing piece finally happy?**
(Possible answer: It needed to learn to be happy with itself and roll alone, no longer waiting around for someone else to make it happy.)

Finish the illustration by saying, **No boy will ever complete you! Even when you try really, really hard, and it feels as if he's fulfilling your missing piece at first, he can't do so forever. Only God can make you roll alone happily. Then when a boy comes along, you can be happy together. And when he leaves, you can still be happy.**

Other illustration options if you don't use the book—

▷ **Imagine you're playing the game Jenga. You take several pieces out of the tower. Most of them don't matter. Finally, you pull out the one piece that was holding the whole structure together. In your life the one piece is Christ. You can have boyfriends, but without Christ your structure will fall.**

▷ **Have you seen those huge, inflatable jumping toys and games? Some are to jump in, some to climb in, others are for sumo wrestling, etc. You plug in the inflatable item, and it inflates because of a huge fan blowing continuously. It stays inflated until you turn the fan off. But if you take the inflatable outside one day to play with and don't plug it in, what fun would it be? It might still bounce around a bit, but until you plug into the main source of power, it won't serve the purpose it was intended for. Dating's the same way. It can be so fun and great but when we spend all our time and energy on boys and forget to keep God as our main source of power, dating won't serve its intended purpose.**

After using the book or one of the other illustrations, say, **Christ has to be our source of fulfillment. Boys can sure be great and a lot of fun when we're happy with ourselves as we already are. Otherwise, dating can be painful and destroy our self-worth.**

Are you ready to date?

Ask, **Are you ready to date? You should ask yourself a few questions before you reach your conclusion.**

Reality Check

9. What do my <u>parents</u> say?

Explain, **If it's fine with your parents for you to date, then ask what they think of the particular guy you want to date. When you ask for their opinions about who you date, you'll be opening the door to more trust and freedom in your dating experiences. If you're hiding the fact you're dating a certain guy from your parents, you shouldn't be dating him.**

Reality Check

10. What's my <u>hurry</u>? Is he even a close friend yet?

Ask, **What are some of the qualities you look for in a good friendship—with anyone of either gender? How long does it take to build a good friendship?**

After some answers say, **What was the first reason we mentioned about why God placed in us a desire to find love? To get married and have children. Then ask, What's the point of dating?** *(possible answers: fun, training, finding out what you like and don't like in males)*

After some discussion say, **Are you getting married and having children now—or anytime soon? So what's the rush?**

Continue, **Besides, if a guy isn't worth being friends with for a long time first, why would he be worth dating? If he doesn't even make the friend cut, he's certainly not dating material.**

Reality Check

11. Does this guy fit my "<u>list</u>"?

Explain, **Do you even know what you want the guy you marry someday to be like? What are your standards? You'll want to make a list of all the qualities you want in a guy. If you don't know what you're looking for, you'll never find it. You'll get a chance to start this list in this week's Soul Work.**

Reality Check

12. **Proverbs 4:23 warns: Above all else you should <u>guard</u> your heart.**

   Ask, **What do you think this verse means in this context of dating?**

   After some answers say, **You're valuable. Some girls feel as if they have to date every guy who comes along. Others give in to whatever the guy wants to do physically. You don't owe these boys anything! Just because a boy shows interest in you doesn't mean you need to go out with him. You are a gift and a prized possession to be held in high regard. You deserve the best. If a guy doesn't meet your standards or the qualities you list, don't get rid of the list—get rid of the guy.**

Reality Check

13. **Am I a stronger and <u>godlier woman</u> when I'm around him?**

   In the book *For Such a Time as This*, Lisa Ryan tells a story on pages 50 to 52. She decides to attend a party one night in college. She wants to go mostly because a guy she knows will be there. After she arrives, she feels out of place, so she grabs a can of beer to hold for the effect—to look as if she fits in.

> **Then I heard the voice of one of the guys at the party. "Lisa, what are you doing here?" His question caught me off guard. I wasn't sure how to respond. He was a nice guy, and I could tell he was not being mean-spirited. He just looked perplexed. Then, like a big brother, he sat me down and said, "Lisa, you don't belong here." He asked if I had my car or if I needed a ride home. He walked me out and I left—just like that.**
>
> **In that moment, I heard God's voice through that young man: *Lisa, you have been set apart.***

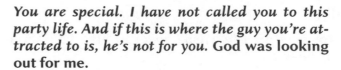

You are special. I have not called you to this party life. And if this is where the guy you're attracted to is, he's not for you. **God was looking out for me.**

Looking back, I realized I needed to understand who I was as a child of God and his destiny for my life.

Then say, **You are a child of God. A princess. Are you acting in a way that's becoming of a princess? Does being around the guy you like cause you to be more like Christ or more like a desperate, lost person?**

Reality Check

14. Am I content <u>without</u> a boyfriend?

Specialty: Movie Clip

Show *Can't Hardly Wait* clip (start at chapter 9 and fast-forward to the piano scene, 36:45, and stop where she says, "I don't know me as anyone else." 38:21).

After the clip say, **When we put too much focus on guys, we can stray from who we are. So ask yourself the big question: "Am I content without a boyfriend?" How do you feel when you have a boyfriend and how do you feel when you don't? If you *have* to have a boyfriend, you aren't ready for one.**

Continue, **When you're unsure of your S.E.L.F. (skills, experiences, likes, and foundation/personality)—in other words, who you really are inside—and not finding contentment and fulfillment from God, what happens? Just as in our movie clip, you totally lose sight of who you started out to be and become whatever those around you are. You become desperate to have a boyfriend and start to use your female "superpower"—sex appeal and outward appearance—to attract boys instead of relying on who you really are to attract friends...of both genders.**

TAKE OUT

Then give each girl a puzzle piece to take home with these Scripture references written on the back: Proverbs 4:23, Matthew 22:37, and 1 Corinthians 13:4-7. They'll be reminders for your girls that only God can complete their lives.

Distribute the **Soul Work** handouts and **My Dream Man!** sheets and close in prayer.

THE PERFECT MAN

You're on a mission to plan the perfect evening for the perfect man—who you'll also need to find. Using your magazines, find these items, cut them out, and glue them to your paper. The first one to get all the items wins!

▷ An outfit that'll blow your guy out of the water.

▷ Time to accessorize! Find jewelry, shoes, a purse, etc., to your own tastes.

▷ A luscious perfume to turn every nose in your direction.

▷ Speaking of gifts, if he's the perfect man, then of course he brings you a gift. What did he bring you?

▷ A scrumptious meal for two, fulfilling every hunger known to humankind.

▷ We need some real, bona fide love: Find the word love.

▷ You need to go somewhere after that incredibly satisfying meal. You pick what you get to do next—dance, talk in the park, hang out with friends, watch a movie, play games, etc.—and find something representing the activity.

▷ The perfect man is irresistible. Dad catches you getting a good-night kiss on the porch. Find a picture or word describing what your dad is feeling.

▷ That was one romantic date. Find the word romantic, romance, or date.

LIVING COMPLETE: BOYS AND THE SEARCH FOR TRUE LOVE

1. _____ placed those _____ in you.

2. If no women wanted to be loved by men (and vice versa), no one would get _____ and no one would have _____—and then no one would be left on earth.

3. You're not looking for a boyfriend—you're seeking _____.

4. 1 Corinthians 13 is the love chapter in the Bible. Verses 4-7 list things that show true love: Love is _____, kind, does not envy, does not boast, it is not proud, it does not dishonor others, it is not _____, it is not easily angered, it keeps no record of wrong, does not delight in evil but rejoices with truth, always _____, trusts, hopes, and perseveres.

5. Only God can _____ these desires.

6. God _____ love.

7. Matthew 22:37 says, "'Love the Lord your God with all your _____ and with all your _____ and with all your _____.'"

8. God placed those feelings and desires in you to help you keep _____ God.

Are you ready to date?

9. What do my _____ say?

10. What's my _____? Is he even a close friend yet?

11. Does this guy fit my "_____"?

12. Proverbs 4:23 warns: Above all else you should _____ your heart.

13. Am I a stronger and _____ when I'm around him?

14. Am I content _____ a boyfriend?

SOUL WORK

LIVING COMPLETE: BOYS AND THE SEARCH FOR TRUE LOVE

BRAINTEASERS

Grab your favorite drink, your comfiest slippers, and your smartest friend. Use these clues to guess some last names. For example: What's growing out of your head? Answer: Harris (hair is)

1. Two things you do with coffee... _____

2. When a fisherman is telling the size of the fish he caught, you know he's... _____

3. What the hippie said when he was asked what was wrong with his lips... _____

4. A past-tense male... _____

5. What a good mom does when her son comes crying to her with a skinned knee... _____

SOUL WORK QUESTIONS

1. How do you feel about the five questions on dating (numbers 9, 10, 11, 13, and 14 on your Reality Check sheets and listed below)? Are there any you strongly agree or disagree with?

   A. What do my parents say?

   B. What's my hurry? Is he even a close friend yet?

   C. Does this guy fit my "list"?

   D. Am I a stronger and godlier woman when I'm around him?

   E. Am I content without a boyfriend?

2. Do you ever place more importance on boys than God? Circle one: yes no

   (If you say no, you may want to consider how truthful your answer is!)

3. In what ways have you made compromises for boys? This can include how you treated a friend, whether you've disrespected or disobeyed your parents over a guy, cheated in school to impress him, changed your appearance for him, etc.

4. Ask your parents what they love most about each other. If your parents are divorced, explain that you're thinking about relationships and wondering what they'd consider vital characteristics in someone to love.

5. Start making a list the qualities of your ideal man you want to marry someday. Use your My Dream Man! sheet for this list. You can add to it over the next week and also over the next few years.

MY DREAM MAN!

This is a character description of the man I would like to marry someday. List all the qualities you would like your future husband to have.

If the guy I'm dating or want to date doesn't have these character traits, I'll get rid of the guy, not this list.

_____

(sign your name here)

CHAPTER SEVEN

LIVING AS A WOMAN: A LOOK INTO THE FUTURE

INGREDIENTS

Several spoons, *The Rookie* DVD, *Parenthood* DVD, "I Hope You Dance" song by Lee Ann Womack on *I Hope You Dance* CD, blank CDs (one per girl), a marker that will write on CDs

REVIEW SOUL WORK

Here are the answers to last week's brainteasers:

1. Brewster (brew and stir)
2. Lyon (lyin')
3. Chapman (chapped, man)
4. Boyd ("boy-ed")
5. Patterson (pat her son)

APPETIZER: SPOON-READING GAME

Have all the girls sit on the floor. They choose one girl to take the pile of spoons and create letters to spell any word—while you're out of the room. Your job is to enter the room, examine the spoon word, and pick out which girl arranged the letters. Here's the key. Before the game pull one of the girls aside to be your secret prompter—she should keep an eye on the "spoon writer" and sit in exactly the same style and position as that girl. Just glance at your prompter a bit, look for the girl in the matching pose, and come up with the right name. Do this several times to show how brilliant you are. Should the group choose your secret prompter to spell a word with the spoons, agree beforehand what word she'll spell, then you'll know to choose her.

QUESTIONS AND COMMENTARY

After the game say, **I used my sixth sense to read the spoons; now you get to use your sixth sense and look into your future. I want to give you exactly seven minutes and 20 seconds to answer questions 1A through M on your Reality Check sheets.**

Reality Check

High school

1. In high school I want to...

    A. get a job. true/false

    B. be allowed to go on dates. true/false

    C. drive places without Mom and Dad. true/false

    Beyond high school

    D. Right after high school I'm planning to...

    ...join the Army, attend college, party, sleep, get married, continue whatever job I'm already working at; who said I'd finish high school?

    E. When I "grow up," I want to be...

    F. My ideal age for getting married is...

    G. I want to be a virgin when I get married. true/false

    H. From My Dream Man! list last week, these are the two most important things to me:

    I. I'd like to have___kids, and I'd like them to be spaced out by___ years. (If you wouldn't like to have kids, write 0.)

    J. I'd rather be a stay-at-home mom/working mom.

    K. When I'm an adult, I will/won't go to church.

    L. I will/won't pay all of my bills on time.

    M. Other things I want everyone to know about my future—

After your girls have finished, ask, **What's the likelihood all these things will come to pass?** After some answers ask, **What's going to determine whether these things really happen or not?** After some answers share point two.

Reality Check

2. **The real mark of becoming a woman is being <u>responsible</u> and making responsible choices.**

Say, **Let's look a little deeper into your future. You've heard this question before: "What do you want to be when you grow up?" I want you as a group to shout out all the jobs women stereotypically are supposed to have.** *(possible answers: cosmetologist, secretary, maid/housecleaner, nanny, elementary school teacher, cashier, flight attendant, nurse, etc.)*

After some answers say, **Now don't misunderstand me. Nothing's wrong with any of these jobs. To say these jobs aren't significant isn't only untrue—it's not even the point. The point is they're stereotypically considered women's jobs.**

Now ask, **What jobs are stereotypically considered men's jobs?** *(possible answers: scientist, math or science teacher, police officer, soldier, politician, engineer, astronaut, construction worker, professional athlete, etc.)*

After you receive some answers, ask, **Why do so many jobs seem to be gender-related?**

Following some discussion say, **Traditionally, men have been seen as having more muscles and brains. Women, as you know, have been valued for their bodies and caretaking abilities— and anything else we have to offer is a bonus. The stereotype has been, if a man finds a woman who's beautiful and smart, he's thought to have found a rare gem.**

Now say, **The good thing is, our culture has been slowly changing and is more and more viewing women as equal to men in many important ways. We've had a woman as the captain of the space shuttle, and some states have women as governors. Women have been doctors and lawyers and scientists for a long time; they're in all sorts of military positions. The point is—you can do anything you want. The question is—*how do you get there?***

Reality Check

3. Dream <u>big</u>!

Tell them, **Jesus says if we trust God even the smallest bit—the size of a mustard seed, in fact—we can do anything (Matthew 17:20). Why do you think Jesus uses the mustard seed as an example?**

After some guesses say, **When Jesus talks about this in the Bible, he uses the example of a mustard seed because it was the smallest seed planted in his time. Yet when harvest time came, it was one of the largest plants. His point is this: If you start out trusting him even the smallest bit, he can turn your trust into the most amazing thing imaginable. He *is* amazing and he can help you reach your goals.**

Continue, **The fun of being in middle school is you have your whole life ahead of you. Nothing is stopping you from reaching your dreams.**

Reality Check

4. **Jeremiah 29:11 says, "'For I know the plans I have for you,' declares the LORD, 'plans to prosper you and not to harm you, plans to give you hope and a future.'"**

   Say, **And you know what?**

Reality Check

5. **"What, then, shall we say in response to these things? If God is for us, who can be against us?" (Romans 8:31)**

   Next say, **God has a purpose for putting you on this earth. God has big dreams for you. And with God as your biggest cheerleader, how can you go wrong? Your job is to listen to God to see what's in store for you. How does God tell you?**

   After some answers say, **God doesn't make it too hard for us, yet if we aren't paying attention, it can seem as though God is being silent. One major way to know what God has planned for you is to look at your S.E.L.F. (skills, experiences, likes, and foundation/personality). Another way is to look for opportunities to show God's love by serving others. The next way is to ask God. Let God tell you instead of relying on everyone and everything around you.**

Specialty: Movie Clip

Show *The Rookie* clip (31:17 "Anybody want to tell me how..." to 38:10 when the speed limit sign changes from 76 to 96). This is a seven-minute clip. You can watch the whole thing, or to make it shorter you can stop right after the coach is done talking to his team. This movie is about a baseball coach considering a second chance at achieving his dream, which he'd given up on long ago. He's encouraging his team by telling them if they'd just start dreaming for something bigger than what they're doing now, they could achieve great things. But their minds are set on failing. The message is, dream big!

After the clip say, **We all have big dreams when we're young. So what happens? Many people never try to be who they wanted to be early in life and give up on their dreams. When does the change happen?**

Then say, **Right now. Middle school. Too often people your age don't think in the long term when making decisions. They don't consider how their choices now will affect them later in life. Our choices do matter. But in middle school we get busy having fun and being cool—we often stop dreaming and working toward those dreams.**

Reality Check

6. **What you do as a middle school student <u>matters</u> for what you do later in life.**

Continue, **Let's see how this works out in real life.**

Specialty: Scenarios/Questions

Ask three of your girls to take turns reading the following three scenarios (which appear on their **Reality Check** sheets). After each scenario is read, ask your group the questions after it in your leader script and hold a discussion.

Reality Check

Scenario #1: Stacy wants to be a lawyer when she grows up; however, she's failing math and science classes. Her parents get all worked up over it, but she hates math and science. "They have nothing to do with being a lawyer anyway, so what's the big deal?" she says.

▷ **Why do Stacy's parents get all worked up?**

▷ **How will her grades affect her attending the college she wants to go to?**

▷ **What life trend is Stacy creating by not trying hard in her classes?** (*Possible answers: She's following the idea that if you don't enjoy something, you don't have to bother working hard at it. So she's making studying not important.*)

- ▷ **How will this affect different areas in her life?**
- ▷ **What are the benefits of working hard in school?**
- ▷ **What can Stacy do to get back on track to becoming a lawyer?**
- ▷ **How would thinking long term help make her decision easier?**

Scenario #2: Amber has decided she wants to get married and have kids. As a child she went to church, and she loved singing the songs, doing crafts, and all the stuff kids get to do. She's sure she wants her future kids to enjoy the same experience. Amber is dating a guy named Jason who thinks she's a little weird for wanting this for her kids. In fact, Jason thinks the idea of going to church sounds boring. He likes having an extra day to sleep in on the weekends.

- ▷ **If Amber and Jason someday get married, what conflicts will they have in regards to churchgoing?**
- ▷ **If Amber takes the kids to church by herself, what is Jason teaching the kids?**
- ▷ **If Amber wants to marry a guy who loves Jesus, what's she doing wrong now?**
- ▷ **What can Amber do to get back on track to a future lifestyle that'll include going to church as a family?**
- ▷ **How would thinking long term help Amber?**

Scenario #3: Madalyn asks her parents if she can borrow $10 to go to a movie with her friends. Her mom tells her no because Madalyn never pays her parents back. Madalyn yells at her mom and storms off to her room. All of her friends' parents pay for this stuff. Madalyn can't understand why her parents are any different.

- ▷ **Why is Madalyn mad?**
- ▷ **Why would her mom say no? Is that a valid reason/does the reason make sense?**
- ▷ **Do you think Madalyn's mom is helping her?**
- ▷ **What valuable lesson is Madalyn learning that will help her in the long term?**
- ▷ **What can Madalyn do to help her relationship with her parents as well as prepare herself for the real world?**

▷ **How would thinking long term help Madalyn be wise with her money?**

After the last question has been discussed, say, **Madalyn needed to have some help learning to become responsible to pay her debts; Stacy needed to learn to get her schoolwork done and think long term; and as with Amber, it wouldn't make sense for you to date a guy who doesn't have the same values as you.**

Go on, **Each choice is a tug-of-war. You're either closer or farther away to pulling your opponent into the pit with each step.**

Reality Check

7. **Your choices will <u>get</u> you where you want to go or they'll take you <u>farther</u> away. Only you can decide whether your dreams come true.**

Explain, **The bad news is, whether we're young or old, we all make bad choices at some point or another. Sometimes these choices have small consequences and other times they're huge. What you need to know is: God's bigger than your biggest problem—and while a lot of big problems can hit us in life, the biggest are sin and death. But check this out.**

Reality Check

8. **John 10:10 tells us that Jesus has "come that they may have life, and have it to the full."**

Say, **Circle "have it to the full." Jesus doesn't promise we'll have it easy, but we can have joy in him. We can be forgiven and alive. And that's having life to the full.**

Reality Check

9. **It's never too <u>late</u> to reach your dreams.**

Next say, **It may not be easy, but never give up on what you believe God's calling you to do.**

Leader Note: *If you only showed part of* The Rookie *clip earlier, you could show the rest of the clip here with the speed limit sign changing* *if you have time. In either case now say,* **Remember our clip of *The Rookie?* Even though the coach thought his chances were long gone years before, he just had to take a shot at it and not give up on his dream.**

Our Weakness/God's Grace

Ask, **In the Bible Paul describes his weaknesses as a good thing— how could that possibly be true?**

After you receive some answers, say, **It's not like we should try to keep our weaknesses—rather we can think of them as a way for God to be seen through us when God helps us overcome or deal with our weaknesses. In 2 Corinthians 12:9 Paul describes what Jesus tells him: "'My grace is sufficient for you, for my power is made perfect in weakness.' Therefore I will boast all the more gladly about my weaknesses, so that Christ's power may rest on me."**

Specialty: Movie Clip

Show *Parenthood* clip (1:49 "I love you" to 1:56 when Gil hugs his wife). Grandma tells about how many people choose the easy way in life, but she would rather—in all her wisdom of life—choose the harder but more enjoyable life. Tell your group, **The point is not to let a few risks, the fear of failure, or having to work hard stop you from having your dreams come true. Dreams are always worth the hard work.**

TAKE OUT

"I Hope You Dance" by Lee Ann Womack is not a Christian song, but its message fits with this lesson: Sometimes you just have to go for it. (Beware: The song has the word *hell* in it. If you choose to use the song, you may want to avoid passing out the lyrics—the most important thing is to gauge your youth group and church body as to whether playing this song is appropriate for your girls. You can find the lyrics on the Internet if you need to review them.)

If you choose to use the song, the following will help you discuss it with your girls; if you choose not to use the song, skip down to the Final Project Option.

Say, **This song isn't really talking about dancing. But it is talking about taking a risk for the sake of making your dreams come true and enjoying life. All the things we talked about at the beginning of our lesson that you want to do in life someday can come true. You just need to make choices to support where you want to go in life. Sometimes those choices involve taking risks. Those risks may mean you go out of your comfort zone or tap into your "hate it but do it" center where you do something not fun now just for the sake of helping your dreams come true. Examples of these activities include studying hard, paying back your parents for money you borrow, and dating only certain types of guys even when others are "so cute." And some of the risks will be purely fun and exciting. Just remember who you eventually want to be and make choices—whether hard, easy, scary, etc.—to help you become that person.**

Now give each girl a blank CD with the words *I hope you dance* written on the CD. Challenge the girls to hang the CDs somewhere they'll see them to remind them to take the hard road sometimes and not give up on their dreams for the future.

FINAL PROJECT OPTION

Leader's Note

Many of you have taught both *Young Woman of God* books. You've done a lot of work with these girls. Some of them haven't done their **Soul Work**, but they've shown up for some of the lessons—and that's great. Others haven't done the **Soul Work** but have shown up most of the time, which is even better. Others of you have students who've been there for the lessons and completed most or even all of the **Soul Work**. These girls have no doubt had some transformations in their mindsets and in their lives.

As you've seen, we've talked about some very relevant things for these girls in their everyday lives. My prayer is we've helped set the girls up for the rest of their lives with a firmer foundation to be stronger women, more independent, and proud of who they are as God made them. This final project gives them an opportunity to show who they are and what they've discovered about themselves using their unique talents and abilities. It incorporates everything in the two books for one big presentation. This is a lot to ask of a middle school student, yet doing this final project has always been an incredible experience for the girls I've ministered to. I've heard poems, seen bulletin boards and poster boards, and even just read written summaries. They should take on their final projects according to their own commitment levels—some may even choose not to take part. But some will choose to "dance." This just gives them one more opportunity to do that.

If you choose this option for your group, count it as their **Soul Work** for the week and have your girls present their final projects during the session the last week—that is the study. If you choose not to go the final project route, regular **Soul Work** is available. In fact, a whole Week-Eight session is part of this curriculum if you choose not to do the final projects. Either way, use the week after you're all done to have a party for your girls and celebrate all their hard work.

Presenting the final project option

Say, **Can you believe we're at the end of our series? You've all worked so hard and I'm so proud of you. Next week we'll be celebrating all your hard work, giving away prizes, and presenting your final projects. FINAL PROJECTS?! WHAT ARE *THEY*?**

Continue, **We've spent many weeks discovering who God created you to become. We've looked into just about every aspect of your life. Now I want to sit back and let you teach me. I've asked you to keep all your notes, Soul Work, and any other stuff, such as letters from your parents. You're going to present yourself to the group. How you do this is up to you. Our week on Living as My S.E.L.F. will be very helpful. If you're good at writing, write a poem, a story, or maybe just a report about who you are, what you've learned about yourself, and your plans for your future life. If you're an artsy person, illustrate your own story, do a painting, or make something to put in your room. If you're an organized person who likes order and lists, make a bulletin board–style presentation about yourself and what you've learned. If you love acting, write and perform a skit about yourself. If you're good with technology, make a video or a PowerPoint presentation. These are just a few ideas. Ask your parents for more ideas. And I'll do my best to help you. If you need supplies to make your stuff, feel free to ask.**

Distribute the **Final Project** handouts and close in prayer.

REGULAR ENDING (NON-FINAL PROJECT OPTION)

Say, **Next week is our last meeting about living as a young woman of God. You've done really well and have worked very hard. Let's finish strong and learn as much as we can about ourselves while we have time.**

Distribute the **Soul Work** handouts and close in prayer.

REALITY CHECK

LIVING AS A WOMAN: A LOOK INTO THE FUTURE

High school

1. In high school I want to...

    A. get a job. true/false

    B. be allowed to go on dates. true/false

    C. drive places without Mom and Dad. true/false

Beyond high school

    D. Right after high school I'm planning to...

    ...join the Army, attend college, party, sleep, get married, continue whatever job I'm already working at; who said I'd finish high school?

    E. When I "grow up," I want to be _____.

    F. My ideal age for getting married is _____.

    G. I want to be a virgin when I get married. true/false

    H. From My Dream Man! list last week, these are the two most important things to me:

    I. I'd like to have _____ kids, and I'd like them to be spaced out by _____ years. (If you wouldn't like to have kids, write 0.)

    J. I'd rather be a stay-at-home mom/working mom.

    K. When I'm an adult, I will/won't go to church.

    L. I will/won't pay all of my bills on time.

    M. Other things I want everyone to know about my future—

2. The real mark of becoming a woman is being _____ and making responsible choices.

3. Dream _____!

4. Jeremiah 29:11 says, "'For I know the plans _____ have for you,' declares the LORD, 'plans to prosper you and not to harm you, plans to give you hope and a _____.'"

5. "What, then, shall we say in response to these things? If God is _____ us, who can be against us?" (Romans 8:31)

6. What you do as a middle school student _____ for what you do later in life.

   Scenario #1: Stacy wants to be a lawyer when she grows up; however, she's failing math and science classes. Her parents get all worked up over it but she hates math and science. "They have nothing to do with being a lawyer anyway, so what's the big deal?" she says.

   Scenario #2: Amber has decided she wants to get married and have kids. As a child she went to church, and she loved singing the songs, doing crafts, and all the stuff kids get to do. She's sure she wants her future kids to enjoy the same experience. Amber is dating a guy named Jason who thinks she's a little weird for wanting this for her kids. In fact, Jason thinks the idea of going to church sounds boring. He likes having an extra day to sleep in on the weekends.

   Scenario #3: Madalyn asks her parents if she can borrow $10 to go to a movie with her friends. Her mom tells her no because Madalyn never pays her parents back. Madalyn yells at her mom and storms off to her room. All of her friends' parents pay for this stuff. Madalyn can't understand why her parents are any different.

7. Your choices will _____ you where you want to go or they'll take you _____ away. Only you can decide whether your dreams come true.

8. John 10:10 tells us Jesus has "come that they may have life, and have it to the full."

9. It's never too _____ to reach your dreams.

FINAL PROJECT

Brainteaser

Here's a quick brainteaser. A man in New York reads a small article in the paper about a Midwestern man and his wife. The article states that while on a skiing trip to the Swiss Alps, the wife had an accident and died. The man reading the article in New York immediately phones the police and tells them he has proof the woman's death wasn't an accident. Later that evidence is instrumental in the conviction of the husband for premeditated murder. Who was the man in New York and how did he know the wife's death wasn't an accident?

Final project

I know this is going to use some brainpower. I have confidence in you and I'm excited to see what you'll come up with. Remember, I'll do anything you need to help you out. The best place to start is to look through your Reality Check outlines and your Soul Work sheets. These will help you remember what we've talked about as well as some of the things you may've discovered about yourself. And here are some questions to get you thinking as well.

▷ How do I feel about how women are represented in our culture?

▷ Who are some of the women I look up to and why?

▷ What are some long-term goals I've set for myself?

▷ What are the boundaries and rewards I have to help me?

▷ How do I feel about my body?

▷ What are some areas I'm working on to have a better body image?

▷ What masks do I wear?

▷ What did I write in my letter to myself that I might like to share?

▷ What's something my parents wrote in their letter(s) to me that I might like to share?

▷ What are some of my skills?

▷ What are some experiences that have shaped my life?

▷ What are some things I like to do?

▷ What's my foundation (or my personality traits)?

▷ How do I feel knowing God's name is autographed on me?

▷ How do my feelings and emotions affect me?

▷ How well do I handle my emotions?

▷ What am I working on to stay in control of my emotions?

▷ How am I doing with renewing my mind to the mind of Christ?

▷ How does journaling help me deal with my feelings and emotions?

▷ Am I a good friend?

▷ Do I show the traits of a good friend? Sister? Daughter?

▷ How do I feel toward my parents?

▷ How well do I honor and obey my parents?

▷ How does God's promise to me help when I'm dealing with my parents?

▷ How do I treat my siblings?

▷ What am I working on to improve my relationship with them?

▷ Do I put too much value on what boys think of me?

▷ Am I making good choices regarding boyfriends?

▷ Am I using my body in appropriate ways?

▷ Do I use the "five questions to ask myself" in a relationship?

▷ What are some things I put on My Dream Man! list?

▷ What do I want to do with my future?

▷ What career do I want to pursue?

▷ What kind of family do I want?

▷ How have my opinions, values, and/or goals changed through the Young Woman of God classes?

▷ What's keeping me from reaching my goals?

These are just some thoughts. Remember, this project can be done any way you come up with. You may add more things or not include any of these things. God created us each in a different way. Next week we'll be celebrating some of the different talents and the uniqueness of each other. Have fun!

LIVING AS A WOMAN: A LOOK INTO THE FUTURE

Everyone is always saying kids try to grow up too fast—well, this week is your chance to be all grown up for a week. So let's get to it. Go find the most adult-looking pen in your house and maybe a coffee....

Brainteaser

Here's a quick brainteaser. A man in New York reads a small article in the paper about a Midwestern man and his wife. The article states that while on a skiing trip to the Swiss Alps, the wife had an accident and died. The man reading the article in New York immediately phones the police and tells them he has proof the woman's death wasn't an accident. Later that evidence is instrumental in the conviction of the husband for premeditated murder. Who was the man in New York and how did he know the wife's death wasn't an accident?

Soul Work questions

1. This week we looked at some things you'd like to have be true in the future. How would you like to be in high school (sports, grades, music, arts, friends, faith, family, character, personality, etc.)?

2. How do you see yourself in 15 years?

3. What are some dreams you have for yourself that maybe you haven't told anyone because they seem too big?

4. What are some choices and/or risks you need to take to help you be the person you want to be in 15 years or to make your "too-big" dream become a reality?

5. Share your dream with one person and ask her to help you make choices to work toward making the dream a reality.

CHAPTER EIGHT

LIVING AS THE REAL ME

INGREDIENTS

The Cider House Rules DVD, a copy of the story "A Parable about the King" by Beth Moore to read to the group, A Parable about the King handouts, paper crowns or tiaras (one for each girl)

Leader Note: *There's an optional letter to send home to parents. The gist: These girls are princesses, but our culture doesn't treat them like princesses. So we're encouraging Dad, when possible, to take his girl on a father-daughter date. The purpose is to show the girls how they should be treated—as princesses. If anyone ever treats them as less, they need to walk away.*

REVIEW SOUL WORK

Answer to last week's brainteaser: The man who calls the police is a travel agent. He knows it wasn't an accident because the husband had bought only a one-way plane ticket for his wife but a round-trip ticket for himself.

APPETIZER: ROYALTY REFLECTION QUIZ

Tell your girls that you want to begin this week by talking about royalty. To do so, they'll each take the Royalty Reflection Quiz at the top of their Reality Check sheets. After a few minutes go over the quiz and have your girls shout out their answers.

▷ What do you think it's like to be a king? *(Possible answers: Kings are so rich; they have people bowing down to them; maybe their faces are on their countries' money; stressful; they have boats, swimming pools, more money than they know what to do with.)*

▷ What kinds of privileges do people of royalty get? *(Possible answers: Everything's free. They can do and say whatever they want. They get only the best food and drinks, clothes, cars, houses, etc.)*

▷ What do you imagine life is like for kings and other royalty? *(Possible answers: They're spoiled, rich. They can get whatever they want, whenever they want, however they want, etc. They have lots of "friends" because they have lots of money.)*

▷ How do you think being royalty affects people's behavior? *(Possible answers: They could go either way. They could act crazy because they have so much power, or they could act more responsible because they're in charge of so much.)* Leaders, don't let too much out of the bag right here—we'll come back to this one.

▷ Now imagine the children of royalty. What do you think life is like for those kids? *(Possible answers: The best life ever! They get whatever they want—the best toys, games, etc. Paris Hilton is one of those kids. When her parents die, she's one of the main heirs or receivers of the inheritance. Whoa!)*

QUESTIONS AND COMMENTARY

After the quiz share point one.

Reality Check

1. **The Bible says we—you and I—are <u>daughters</u> of a King as well.**

   Say, **Let's talk about what this means. If my guess is correct, your moms and dads aren't kings and queens. So how are you royalty? Let's watch a movie clip to help explain how this works a little.**

Specialty: Movie Clip

Show *The Cider House Rules* clip (chapter 5 or start at 13:42 when a car drives up to the orphanage and play 'til 15:50, "Only the right people can have you"). This provides a good illustration about being adopted or chosen.

After the clip say, **This video clip is great! Because this is the idea with you. When you think of kids in an orphanage, what kinds of kids do you think of?**

After some answers say, **We usually think of kids no one wants. The leftovers. But that actually isn't the case. People all over the country pay thousands of dollars to adopt children. The problem is, it takes too long to adopt them. Sometimes we think we're worthless and if people knew who we really are, they wouldn't like us, let alone adopt us if we were orphans. However, it's not true. God does know your deepest secrets and...**

Reality Check

2. **God has chosen you. You've been <u>adopted</u>.**

Now say, **You were bought with the priceless life of Jesus. God gave Jesus' life in exchange for adopting you.**

Reality Check

3. **Since God is the King of the world, you are the <u>princess</u> of the world!**

Then say, **You're royalty. Pretty cool. 1 Peter 2:9 says, "But you are a chosen people, a royal priesthood, a holy nation, God's special possession, that you may declare the praises of him who called you out of darkness into his wonderful light."**

In the Royalty Reflection Quiz, we asked the question, "How do you think being royalty affects people's behavior?" Let's look at how being royalty should affect *our* behavior.

At one time we too acted like fools. We didn't obey God. We were tricked. We were controlled by all kinds of longings and pleasures. We were full of evil. We wanted what belongs to others. People hated us, and we hated one another. But the kindness and love of God our Savior appeared. He saved us. It wasn't because of the good things we had done. It was because of his mercy. He saved us by washing away our sins. We were born again. The Holy Spirit gave us new life. God poured out the Spirit on us freely because of what Jesus Christ our Savior has done. His grace made us right with God. So now we have received the hope of eternal life as God's children. You can trust that saying. Those things are important. Treat them that way. Then those who have trusted in God will be careful to commit themselves to doing what is good. Those things are excellent. They are for the good of everyone. (Titus 3:3-8, NIrV)

Explain, **Okay, that's a lot of info—we'll break it down a bit. Verse 3 says, "At one time we too acted like fools. We didn't obey God. We were tricked. We were controlled by all kinds of longings and pleasures. We were full of evil. We wanted what belongs to others. People hated us, and we hated one another." At what point of a person's life is Paul referring to in this verse?**

After some answers say, **He's talking about before we were Christians. Or in terms of royalty, before we were adopted into our inheritance.**

Listen to verses 4-6:

But the kindness and love of God our Savior appeared. He saved us. It wasn't because of the good things we had done. It was because of his mercy. He saved us by washing away our sins. We were born again. The Holy Spirit gave us new life. God poured out the Spirit on us freely because of what Jesus Christ our Savior has done.

Ask, **What is the kindness and love of God our Savior?** *(possible answer: Jesus dying on the cross)*

After a few answers say, **Jesus saves us, rather than all the good things we do as Christians. It's great to pray and ask forgiveness, but Jesus died for our sins. His blood is what saves us, not our prayers. If our prayers had that much power, then we could save ourselves. But we can't. Our response is to accept his mercy and grace. Then Jesus gives us new life. This doesn't mean we go back into our moms and try for a second round at birth. And your mom is thanking God for sure on that one!**

Reality Check

4. **Titus 3:7 says, "His grace made us right with God. So now we have received the hope of eternal life as God's <u>children</u>."**

   Now say, **If we ask Jesus' forgiveness and trust in his sacrifice for us, we become acceptable to God. We're given the "hope of eternal life"—life in heaven—as princesses. Make sure to let the girls know if they want to talk more about salvation, you're available.**

   Continue, **Verse 8 says, "You can trust that saying. Those things are important. Treat them that way." It goes on to say...**

Reality Check

5. **"Then those who have trusted in God will be careful to <u>commit</u> themselves to doing what is good. Those things [that] are excellent. They are for the good of everyone." (Titus 3:8, NIrV)**

   Now say, **This is a pretty important verse. Have you ever heard this phrase?**

Reality Check

6. **With privilege comes <u>responsibility</u>.**

   Say, **President John F. Kennedy said that. What do you think it means in relation to the verse I just read?**

   After you receive some answers, say, **Christ purchased you—just so he could set you free. He paid for you with his blood and his life so you could have eternal life. That is important, and...**

Reality Check

7. **If you truly <u>understand</u> who you are, a child of God who Christ died for, you'll act differently.**

Now say, **Maybe you're thinking, "But I'm obviously a pretty good person. I'm at church, aren't I?"** Well, yes. Coming to church is great and a good start. You're growing. Some of you aren't growing, however. Just coming to church doesn't make you godly. Check out this important verse.

Reality Check

8. [Jesus says,] **"I know your deeds, that you are neither cold nor hot. I wish you were either one or the other! So, because you are <u>lukewarm</u>—neither hot nor cold—I am about to spit you out of my mouth." (Revelation 3:15-16)**

   Ask, **What do you think this verse means by hot and cold and lukewarm?**

   After you get some answers say, **If you're trying to grow, that's great and this verse doesn't apply to you. But if you're doing your own thing and being lukewarm—you're being a hypocrite and not helping God. That's not why he died. This is what "with privilege comes responsibility" means. I've also heard someone say, "I'd be a Christian if I ever saw one." His point was, many people claim to be Christians but few actually act like Christ. If we fully understand what Jesus did for us, our actions are a tribute of thanks. Yet so many of us live sinful lives and don't care. What a slap in his face.**

   Continue, **The president and kings and queens can't act with only themselves in mind. They have to do what's good for everyone involved. Titus 3:8 says doing what's good and excellent is "good for everyone." How's that true?**

   After some answers say, **This life isn't just about you. You're a princess, which is a huge honor and privilege, but you have to know...**

Reality Check

9. You <u>represent</u> God whether you want to or not.

Explain, **God is frustrated when people misrepresent him. When you behave as one person at church and another at school, you may think you're getting away with it, but you're misrepresenting Christ. You're being a lukewarm Christian.**

Specialty: Reading (Optional)

(If you're able to secure a copy of this story, you may want to try to fit it into the session.) Say, **Let me read you this story that sums up most of what we've been talking about—"A Parable about the King" by Beth Moore.**

After you've read the story, have your girls complete the accompanying worksheet. They're each supposed to find a partner. They have two minutes to answer the first question together. When their time is up, they need to find a new partner for the next question—and they get two minutes to answer that one, etc. Have your girls find new partners for each of the four questions.

After your girls have had time to complete their worksheets, say, **You are a daughter of the King. You may not behave like it all the time, but...**

Reality Check

10. How you behave doesn't <u>change</u> who you are: You're a child of God.

Now say, **God created you exactly as you are. God loves you and is proud of you. God's desperate to have a deep relationship with you—and all you have to do is choose to have it. That's all. God's not mad at us for all we've done wrong. We're God's children. He loves us and is always there, forgiving us and helping us get back on our feet to try again. You have a special one-way pass to God. VIP, baby!**

Go on, **Do you know the story of the Prodigal Son? The son totally messes up then runs away from home. All the while, his dad is waiting and hoping his son will come home. When he does, Dad throws a party. Think of this as a picture of God's relationship with you: God adopted you. You're God's child. You're God's prized possession, and your picture is in**

God's wallet. You may run away, but God is always waiting for your return. You may mess up a bazillion times, but God can handle it. You need to come to God and remember who you are.

Reality Check

11. You're a princess whether you behave like one or not. Your identity is established. Now what?

    Next say, **Are you going to rise up and take on the responsibility that goes with the privilege of being a princess? This is your life—are you who you want to be?**

TAKE OUT

Now give each girl one of those paper crowns you can get at a certain fast-food hamburger joint (or you can make your own). If you want to splurge since it's the last week, you can also get little pretend tiaras from a drugstore or grocery store. You can find them in the cake decorating aisle for around $3 each. Encourage your girls to keep these crowns as reminders that they're princesses in God's sight—always.

Close in prayer.

OPTIONAL PARENT LETTER

Dear [insert parents' names here],

We've come to the end of this small group series. I'm so proud of your daughter and all the work she's put into her growth and her relationship with Christ.

Mom, I hope you've enjoyed the opportunities to talk with your daughter during her various Soul Work exercises. I've tried hard to keep those lines of communication open as well as helping her to see that you're a real person, too.

I have one more chance to involve you before we finish. This time I'm asking for help from Dad. Galatians 6:9 says, "Let us not become weary in doing good, for at the proper time we will reap a harvest if we do not give up." Raising teenagers can be hard some days—and even harder other days. Don't give up and don't give in! One day your daughter will be grown, and you'll see the harvest of all your hard work. God entrusted you with your daughter. That's a great privilege. In the words of John F. Kennedy, "With privilege comes responsibility."

This week the girls learned they're children of God, which makes them princesses. When I was a teenager, my dad took me on a father-daughter date, and I remember him telling me that if a guy ever treated me with less respect and dignity than he was treating me with right then, the guy had to go.

So my challenge for you, Dad, is to take your daughter on a date. If you're not available, then a grandpa, uncle, or even Mom will do. No Taco Bell drive-through here. You're affirming that your daughter's a princess and showing her how every guy should be treating her. If you don't want a guy to drive up and honk at her to come to the car, let her know. If he should open doors for her, you need to do that. Dads and daughters often don't talk to each other enough; when a time of crisis comes, they have no foundation to build on, so I hope you'll start building that foundation.

You may want to think of some topics to talk about before your dinner. You can tell her about the day you first met her mom and your dating period. Tell her about her birth story. What are your favorite memories of her as a child so far? What are some fun memories of your own childhood? If you need a little more help, remember this—H.E.L.P. = home, education, likes, and people. That's what I do when my kids and I are having a moment of silence. Let me expand on this:

▷ Home: This one may be a little tricky for you, but ask what she thinks about your family and how things are going. What would she change? What does she like?

▷ Education: What's going on at school in general? How are her classes going? Does she like her teachers? What's her favorite part of the day at school? What classes are hard or easy? How can you help make life easier for her at school?

▷ Likes: Ask about the things she does for fun such as sports, music, drama, or other extracurricular activities. You could even ask what she wants to do in her future.

▷ People: Girls always have drama going on with their friends. If you're up for a little real-life soap opera, junior style, then ask away. The key is not to give your daughter more advice or opinions than she wants, or she may never tell you anything again. You can also ask about other people, such as boys and bullies, etc.

Have fun! If you have any questions or need ideas, let me know.

REALITY CHECK

LIVING AS THE REAL ME
Royalty reflection quiz

▷ What do you think it's like to be a king?

▷ What kinds of privileges do people of royalty get?

▷ What do you imagine life is like for kings and other royalty?

▷ How do you think being royalty affects people's behavior?

▷ Now imagine the children of royalty. What do you think life is like for those kids?

Outline

1. The Bible says we—you and I—are _____ of a King as well.

2. God has chosen you. You've been _____.

3. Since God is the King of the world, you are the _____ of the world!

> At one time we too acted like fools. We didn't obey God. We were tricked. We were controlled by all kinds of longings and pleasures. We were full of evil. We wanted what belongs to others. People hated us, and we hated one another. But the kindness and love of God our Savior appeared. He saved us. It wasn't because of the good things we had done. It was because of his mercy. He saved us by washing away our sins. We were

born again. The Holy Spirit gave us new life. God poured out the Spirit on us freely because of what Jesus Christ our Savior has done. His grace made us right with God. So now we have received the hope of eternal life as God's children. You can trust that saying. Those things are important. Treat them that way. Then those who have trusted in God will be careful to commit themselves to doing what is good. Those things are excellent. They are for the good of everyone. (Titus 3:3-8, NIrV)

4. Titus 3:7 says, "His grace made us right with God. So now we have received the hope of eternal life as God's _____."

5. "Then those who have trusted in God will be careful to _____ themselves to doing what is good. Those things [that] are excellent. They are for the good of everyone." (Titus 3:8, NIrV)

6. With privilege comes _____.

7. If you truly _____ who you are, a child of God who Christ died for, you'll act differently.

8. [Jesus says,] "I know your deeds, that you are neither cold nor hot. I wish you were either one or the other! So, because you are _____—neither hot nor cold—I am about to spit you out of my mouth." (Revelation 3:15-16)

9. You _____ God whether you want to or not.

10. How you behave doesn't change _____ you are: You're a child of God.

11. You're a princess whether you behave like one or not. Your identity is established. _____?

WORKSHEET: A PARABLE ABOUT THE KING (OPTIONAL)

Find a partner. You'll have two minutes to answer the first question together. When your time is up, find a new partner for the next question and you'll have two minutes to answer it. Find a new partner to help answer each question.

1. What does it mean to be a daughter of God, a princess of the King?

2. How would remembering you're a princess change your behavior...
    A. ...with your family?

    B. ...with your friends?

    C. ...with boys?

    D. ...when you're alone?

3. Is the person you are every day becoming of a true princess? Why or why not?

4. What do you want or need to change to be the princess God created you to be?